DATE DUE		

921
CLI

3 24571 0900150 7
Abrams, Dennis.

Hillary Rodham
Clinton : politician

Women of Achievement

Hillary Rodham Clinton

Women of Achievement

Susan B. Anthony

Hillary Rodham Clinton

Marie Curie

Ellen DeGeneres

Nancy Pelosi

Rachael Ray

Eleanor Roosevelt

Martha Stewart

Women of Achievement

Hillary Rodham Clinton

POLITICIAN

Dennis Abrams

CHELSEA HOUSE
PUBLISHERS
An imprint of Infobase Publishing

HILLARY RODHAM CLINTON

Chelsea House
An imprint of Infobase Publishing
132 West 31st Street
New York NY 10001

Library of Congress Cataloging-in-Publication Data
Abrams, Dennis, 1960-
  Hillary Rodham Clinton : Politician / Dennis Abrams.
    p. cm. — (Women of achievement)
  Includes bibliographical references and index.
  ISBN 978-1-60413-077-5 (hardcover)
  1. Clinton, Hillary Rodham—Juvenile literature. 2. Presidents' spouses—United States—Biography—Juvenile literature. 3. Legislators—United States—Biography—Juvenile literature. 4. Women legislators—United States—Biography—Juvenile literature. 5. United States. Congress. Senate—Biography—Juvenile literature. 6. Presidential candidates—United States—Biography—Juvenile literature. I. Title. II. Series.

  E887.C55A43 2009
  973.929092—dc22
  [B]
                              2008034639

Chelsea House books are available at special discounts when purchased in bulk quantities for businesses, associations, institutions, or sales promotions. Please call our Special Sales Department in New York at (212) 967-8800 or (800) 322-8755.

You can find Chelsea House on the World Wide Web at http://www.chelseahouse.com

Series design by Erik Lindstrom
Cover design by Ben Peterson

Printed in the United States of America

Bang EJB 10 9 8 7 6 5 4 3 2 1

This book is printed on acid-free paper.

All links and Web addresses were checked and verified to be correct at the time of publication. Because of the dynamic nature of the Web, some addresses and links may have changed since publication and may no longer be valid.

CONTENTS

Following Her Heart

In August 1974, U.S. President Richard Nixon was facing certain impeachment by the House of Representatives on charges of abuse of power, obstruction of justice, and contempt of Congress. Rather than face these charges, however, he unexpectedly resigned the office of the presidency. Hillary Rodham, 26, had been advising the House Judiciary Committee as a member of the impeachment inquiry staff. Now, she was suddenly out of a job and found herself at a crossroads in her career and her life. The choice was this: Should she stay in Washington and continue developing her career? Or, should she follow her heart and join her longtime boyfriend, Bill Clinton, in Fayetteville, Arkansas? There, with Rodham by his side as his closest aide and adviser, Clinton hoped to begin his *own* career in politics. It was not an easy decision for Rodham.

Many considered Rodham to be one of the best and brightest of her generation. If she remained in Washington (or moved to New York City), her career potential, whether in law or politics, seemed almost limitless. Some people, including Democratic political organizer and consultant Betsey Wright, who had moved from Texas to Washington to help guide Rodham's career, were convinced that she was destined to become a U.S. senator, if not eventually the first female president of the United States. These same people felt that, if Rodham moved to Arkansas to assist Clinton, she would be doing so at the expense of her own career.

While today such career aspirations for women seem unexceptional, in 1974, the odds were stacked against Rodham's having a successful career in politics. It is easy to forget, from our current perspective, just how much times have changed regarding the role of women in politics. In 2008, 16 women were serving in the U.S. Senate. In 1974, there were no women in the Senate. (Margaret Chase Smith, the first woman elected in her own right to the office, had retired in 1973.) In 1974, there had never been a serious female candidate for the presidency in the country's nearly 200-year history. But in 1974, people were beginning to get a sense that attitudes were changing. It was in many ways the early peak of the women's liberation movement, and with the increasingly accepted idea of women's equality, nothing seemed impossible. To those who knew her, Hillary Rodham became representative of what women might do in what was still considered a man's world, displaying the promise of great achievements ahead.

A graduate of Wellesley College and Yale Law School, Hillary Rodham had first achieved national media attention with her commencement address at Wellesley, in which she declared that "the challenge now is to practice politics as the art of making what appears to be impossible, possible."[1]

At Yale Law School, she served on the Board of Editors of the *Yale Review of Law and Social Action*, and she worked as a research assistant on the groundbreaking work, *Beyond the Best Interests of the Child*, which furthered her growing interest in the legal rights of children. After graduating from Yale, she published her first scholarly work, "Children Under the Law" in the *Harvard Educational Review*, which examined the legal problems of children who suffered from neglect and abuse. Rodham argued that children were not just minors under the law but "child citizens" and thereby entitled to the same rights under the Constitution as adults.

This article, groundbreaking in its time, has become a classic in the field, and it garnered Rodham a good deal of immediate attention. With its publication, along with her work for the House Judiciary Committee, her future, whether as a lawyer, a children's rights advocate, or a politician, seemed limitless. To many observers, she was now in a position that allowed her to fulfill her life's ambitions: to make change, to make a difference, and to help improve the lives of the less fortunate.

But at the same time, with a world of possibilities before her, Hillary Rodham was also a young woman deeply in love. The object of her affection was William Jefferson Clinton. Bill Clinton, a handsome, charming, intelligent Southerner, was a fellow graduate of Yale Law School. Like Rodham, Clinton also had political dreams, ambitions, and aspirations. As Betsey Wright once said, they "both passionately share the sense that they're supposed to make a difference in this world—and they had that before they met each other."[2]

For Bill Clinton to achieve *his* political goals, however, he could not start in Washington. He would have to build

In 1974, Hillary Rodham *(right)* was working as an attorney on the staff putting together the impeachment case against President Richard Nixon for the House Judiciary Committee. When Nixon resigned in August 1974, Rodham's work on the inquiry came to an end. She had a tough decision to make—stay in Washington and pursue her career or move to Arkansas to be with Bill Clinton.

his political career back home in Arkansas. The problem facing Rodham was that, in Arkansas, her career opportunities would be extremely limited. If she moved there with Clinton, she would be giving up her own career to become part of his. It would, in many ways, seem to be a betrayal of everything she had accomplished so far. But, as Rodham says in her autobiography *Living History*, describing her thoughts as she drove with a friend from Washington to Fayetteville, Arkansas:

> I had fallen in love with Bill in law school and wanted to be with him. I knew I was always happier with Bill than without him, and I'd always assumed that I could live a fulfilling life anywhere. . . . So I was driving toward a place where I'd never lived and had no friends or family. But my heart told me I was going in the right direction.[3]

Nearly everybody knows the general outline of what happened after that: As Bill Clinton climbed the political ladder, Hillary Clinton was with him every step of the way. Constantly in the public eye, she has filled many roles: attorney, wife, mother, activist, first lady of the United States, political adviser, U.S. senator, and presidential candidate. In 1988 and 1991, she was listed as one of the 100 most influential lawyers in the United States. The work she has accomplished on behalf of children and the underprivileged, as well as her attempts to make health care available to all Americans, has earned her the respect and admiration of many Americans. Around the world, she is seen as a symbol and strong proponent of women's rights and human rights. She is one of the most widely admired women in the world.

There is a flipside to that picture, however. Because of her forceful views and strong public image, Hillary Clinton has also been ranked among the most disliked and distrusted women in America. Some of the criticism is fair, based on her own errors of political action and judgment. At other times, though, criticism of her crossed the line. Her views have been misrepresented, and she has been criticized for everything from the way she dresses to the way she handles her marriage and personal life. She has been called a ruthless politician, willing to do or say anything to get elected. And sometimes, it seems, the criticism goes off the rails into irrational hatred, as in this description from the Web site www.againsthillary.com: "Hillary Clinton is an ill-tempered, foul-mouthed, hateful, paranoid, and dishonest woman who wants to be the next president of the United States."[4]

Indeed, love or hate her, it seems that there are very few Americans who do *not* have an opinion about Hillary Clinton. She has long been a lightning rod of controversy, representing people's hopes as well as their fears regarding the role of women in today's society.

IN HER OWN WORDS

Hillary Clinton has long been a proponent of women's rights and the role of women in government. In delivering the keynote address at the Vital Voices Conference held in Vienna, Austria, in July 1997, she said:

> We are here to advance the cause of women and to advance the cause of democracy and to make it absolutely clear that the two are inseparable. There cannot be true democracy unless women's voices are heard. There cannot be true democracy unless women are given the opportunity to take responsibility for their own lives.

Truthfully, though, how many people know the real story of Clinton's life? How many know the person behind the headlines? As Clinton herself pointed out in an interview on NBC's *Nightly News*, "I'm probably the most famous person you don't really know."[5] From her Republican upbringing in Illinois, to her student days at Wellesley and Yale, to her marriage to Bill Clinton while attempting to maintain her own identity, to her current role as a political leader, Hillary Clinton has led a life of change. She cannot be easily categorized. She's neither the liberal saint that her supporters see her as nor the evil, power-hungry enemy of the American family that her opponents believe. The truth, as always, is more complicated than that.

Clinton has constantly tried to define her role as both wife and independent woman at a time when the role of women was in constant flux within our society. As Clinton says in the opening paragraph of her autobiography:

> I wasn't born a first lady or a senator. I wasn't born a Democrat. I wasn't born a lawyer or an advocate for women's rights and human rights. I wasn't born a wife or mother. I was born an American in the middle of the twentieth century, a fortunate time and place. I was free to make choices unavailable to past generations of women in my own country and inconceivable to many women in the world today.[6]

What were the choices she made and why did she make them? What did she give up and what did she gain? How do her choices reflect the changing role of women? And perhaps most important, how did her choices set her on the path toward becoming the first serious female candidate for president in U.S. history? How, in other words, did Hillary Rodham become U.S. Senator and presidential candidate Hillary Clinton?

The Early Years

In her autobiography, Hillary Clinton paints a picture of a nearly ideal childhood:

> My parents were typical of a generation who believed in the endless possibilities of America and whose values were rooted in the experience of living through the Great Depression. They believed in hard work, not entitlement; self-reliance, not self-indulgence. This is the world and the family I was born into on October 26, 1947. We were middle-class, Midwestern, and very much a product of our place and time. My mother, Dorothy Howell Rodham, was a homemaker whose days revolved around me and my two younger brothers, and my

father, Hugh E. Rodham, owned a small business. The challenges of their lives made me appreciate the opportunities of my own life even more.[1]

As is often the case, though, reality rarely lives up to the ideal. But as Hillary rightfully points out, her parents did face many challenges in their lives. Her mother, Dorothy, in particular had an extraordinarily difficult childhood, while her father had to escape the influence of a domineering mother. He sold fabric before World War II and trained recruits as a chief petty officer in the U.S. Navy during the war. When the war ended, though, Hugh continued using the same training techniques on his growing family. As journalist Carl Bernstein described it in his book *A Woman in Charge: The Life of Hillary Rodham Clinton*, Hillary's father would issue commands from the comfort of his favorite lounge chair. He would constantly belittle his wife and children, taking little notice of their accomplishments and continuously demanding *more* from them. He called it "character building." To his children, however, he was a man who was nearly impossible to please.

Along with that, he was a man who rarely accepted disagreement. Hugh Rodham was strongly Republican, strongly anti-communist, and unwilling to hear another side of an argument or to admit he might be wrong. "My father was confrontational, completely and utterly so," Hillary's brother, Hugh Jr., said, quoted in *A Woman in Charge*.[2] Hillary and her brothers have said that this was their father's way to ensure that they would be competitive and know how to win a disagreement, but it must have been difficult to grow up under those circumstances.

His need to control the household was absolute; using financial control was one of his most effective tools. Having lived through the Great Depression, he carried with him a need for thrift and an absolute hate of waste. In one often-told story, if Hillary or her brothers left the top off the tube of toothpaste, he would throw it out of the bathroom window and demand that the child go outside and find it—even if they had to dig in the snow. "He was rougher than a corncob and gruff as could be," an acquaintance once said, quoted by Carl Bernstein.[3] But despite his often difficult behavior, Hillary idolized her father and tried every way she could to please him and win his approval, an approval that was rarely granted.

GROWING UP

Dorothy Rodham was a typical 1950s wife and mother, determined that, despite the difficulties of living with her husband, her children would grow up in a loving and supportive environment. She encouraged Hillary to read and took her to the library every week. Rather than watch television, the two played board games together. Dorothy constantly told Hillary to be herself and to avoid caring what others thought about her. "You're unique," she would say. "You can think for yourself. I don't care if everybody's doing it. We're not everybody. You're not everybody."[4]

She also encouraged her daughter to be tough and to stand up for herself. Hugh's fabric business was doing well, and when Hillary was three, the family moved from Chicago to the suburban town of Park Ridge. There, Hillary was the new kid on the block and reluctant to go outside and play because the girl across the street, Suzy O'Callaghan, was always pushing her around. As Hillary remembered in *Living History*, Dorothy would not allow her to give in to her fears and hide inside the house. Instead, she told her daughter, "Go back out there. And if Suzy hits you, you have my permission to hit her back. You have to stand up for yourself. There's no room in this house for cowards." Hillary went outside and returned just a few minutes later, delighted in her victory. "I can play with the boys now. And Suzy will be my friend!"[5] According to Hillary, she still is.

Her mother, who encouraged Hillary to dream big, suggested that she could become the first woman on the Supreme Court. (It was Sandra Day O'Connor who became the first female Supreme Court justice in 1981.) Hillary had dreams, though, of becoming an astronaut and even wrote to NASA at the age of 14 to volunteer. She was told that women need not apply, and she said in *Living History*, "It was the first time I had hit an obstacle I couldn't overcome with hard work and determination, and I was outraged."[6] (It was not until 1983 that Sally Ride became the first American woman to reach outer space.)

Although she was thwarted in her dream of going into space, she still set her sights and aspirations high, owing largely to her mother's constant encouragement. School came easily to Hillary, and she generally brought home straight As from Eugene Field Elementary School. (Typically, though, her father would then suggest that her school was too easy for her.) Wearing thick glasses due to her extreme nearsightedness, with an eagerness to please and a willingness to work hard, she was a typical teacher's pet. Despite all of this, she found it easy to make friends, some of whom she has kept since elementary school.

ALWAYS BUSY

Hillary was more than just a good student. Somewhat surprisingly, given her glasses and studious air, Hillary was also a bit of a tomboy. Growing up in a house with a father and two brothers who were sports fanatics, she played football, baseball, and tennis, although she was, by her own admission, a clumsy athlete.

She was also a Brownie and later a Girl Scout. She marched in Fourth of July parades, helped with food drives, went door to door selling cookies, and as she said in her autobiography, participated in "every other activity that would earn a merit badge or adult approval."[7] She was the leader in her neighborhood: organizing kids in games and sporting events and helping to raise money for charity. In a photograph from her local newspaper, the *Park Ridge Advocate*, she is shown with a group of friends giving to the United Way a bag of money they had raised with a mock Olympics. Even from an early age, she was involved in helping the less fortunate.

She was also developing a keen interest in politics. Her mother was basically a Democrat (although she would never admit it to her husband) who cared deeply about social issues, while Hugh was a dyed-in-the-wool conservative Republican who hated labor unions, was against most government-aid programs, and complained loudly about high taxes. For the time being, Hillary was content to follow in her father's political footsteps as a proud Republican.

OFF TO HIGH SCHOOL

In 1961, Hillary entered Maine East High School. She worked hard, became involved in a wide range of extracurricular activities (student government and the newspaper, various committees, the *It's Academic* quiz show team that appeared on local television), and was considered one of the most popular girls in school. Despite these accomplishments, like most teens, she was being presented with a new set of challenges.

Hillary had moved from a small neighborhood school to a suburban high school with an enrollment of nearly 5,000 students. Suddenly, she was no longer the smartest girl around. To stay near the top of the class, she would have to work and study harder than she ever had before. But her best efforts notwithstanding, she failed to keep her

During the Democratic National Convention in 1992, Hillary Clinton spent some time with her parents, Dorothy and Hugh Rodham, in her hotel room in New York City. Her father was a strict disciplinarian, while her mother was determined that her children would grow up in a loving and supportive environment.

grade-point average high enough to be ranked among the top-10 students in her class.

Her competitive streak and strong need to be the best showed up in other ways. In eleventh grade, she became her class vice president, and the next year she ran for what she called "the presidency." Even at this age, she had a strong sense of campaign tactics. According to Carl Bernstein, she wrote a letter to her youth minister, saying that her opponent's campaign manager was "slinging mud" at her but that "we did not retaliate. We took the high road and talked about motherhood and apple pie."[8] Unfortunately, taking the high road may have cost her the election—she lost decisively. It was an important lesson to her on how elections are won and lost. In another letter, she explained that she had run "against several boys and lost, which did not surprise me but still hurt, especially because one of my opponents told me I was 'really stupid if I thought a girl could be elected president.'"[9]

At the same time, Hillary was also discovering the world of dating and boys. Her father was not excited about this development. He refused to allow her to take dance lessons. He refused to allow her to get a driver's license, telling her that she did not need one; she had a bike. And, perhaps most important to a high school girl already self-conscious about her looks, he refused to pay for the new stylish clothes that would help her fit in with her classmates and make her more comfortable around boys. Even though Hillary tended to hide behind her large glasses and was seen by some boys as "bossy," she had little trouble getting invitations to go on dates.

A NEW INFLUENCE

As Hillary went through her teens, her relationship with her father suffered. They constantly argued about new clothes and dating. Hillary was also beginning to move away from her father in other ways, along both political and religious lines.

Throughout high school, Hillary remained a Republican. Her ninth-grade history teacher, Paul Carlson, a conservative Republican, encouraged Hillary to read Arizona Senator Barry Goldwater's book *The Conscience of a Conservative*. The book so struck Hillary that she wrote a term paper on the American conservative movement, which she dedicated "to my parents, who have always taught me to be an individual."[10] But Hillary's conservatism, with its emphasis on self-reliance and individualism and its belief that the government's role was not to help those who are less fortunate, was soon to collide with her growing sense of what being religious truly meant.

When looking at the life of Hillary Clinton, it is easy to underestimate the importance that religion has played. She does not publicly talk about her faith a great deal, but it has always been there. In many ways, it is impossible to understand Hillary *without* understanding her religious upbringing.

Her family were longtime Methodists, and for the Rodhams, religion was an essential and central part of their life. "[My family] talked with God, walked with God, ate, studied and argued with God," Hillary once said, quoted in *A Woman in Charge*.[11] Hillary believed that the crux of John Wesley's teachings (Wesley founded the Methodist church in the eighteenth century) was that God's love is expressed through good works, which he explained with one simple rule: "Do all the good you can, by all the means you can, in all the ways you can, in all the places you can, at all the times you can, to all the people you can, as long as ever you can."[12] These religious beliefs soon found themselves in opposition to the political ideas that Hillary had learned from her father and teachers such as Paul Carlson. As Hillary points out in her autobiography, she constantly found herself trying to reconcile her father's insistence on self-reliance with her mother's concerns about social justice.

In 1961, the Reverend Donald Jones entered Hillary's life as a youth minister at her church. Through his Sunday and Thursday night Methodist Youth Fellowships, Hillary was introduced to worlds that she had never dreamed of. She read poets like E.E. Cummings and T.S. Eliot, learned about the paintings of Pablo Picasso, and argued about the meaning of Dostoyevsky's great Russian novel, *The Brothers Karamazov*. But beyond that, Jones introduced her to the world that existed outside the privileged white suburb where she was being raised.

He brought the youth fellowship to visit black and Hispanic churches in Chicago. During these meetings, Hillary began to learn and become interested in the growing civil-rights movement in the United States. So when the Reverend Jones announced that he was going to take the group to hear Dr. Martin Luther King Jr. speak at Orchestra Hall in Chicago and then meet him backstage, she was eager to go.

BARRY GOLDWATER

Barry Morris Goldwater (January 2, 1909–May 29, 1998) was a five-term U.S. senator from Arizona, serving from 1953 to 1965 and again from 1969 to 1987, and he was the Republican Party's nominee for president in the 1964 election. He is the politician most often credited with giving rise to the rebirth of the American conservative movement in the 1960s. Indeed, Goldwater was often called "Mr. Conservative."

The grandson of a Polish immigrant who had built a large number of department stores in Arizona, Goldwater joined the U.S. Army Air Corps at the beginning of World War II. By the end of the war, he had risen to the rank of brigadier general. He had long been an opponent of President Franklin D. Roosevelt and his "New Deal" programs to promote economic growth and social reform, strongly believing that the government had no right to encroach on the liberty of the individual. In response, Goldwater joined the Republican Party and in 1952 was elected to the U.S. Senate.

Considered to be on the extreme right of the Republican Party, Goldwater expressed his views in a syndicated newspaper

Some parents refused to allow their children to go to hear Dr. King, believing that he was a "rabble-rouser," a belief that Hugh Rodham also held. Dorothy granted Hillary permission to go, and the experience changed her forever. Combined with her meetings with underprivileged blacks in Chicago, it helped to mold her strongly held belief that the tragedy of racism in the United States was something that had to be put right for the *nation* to be put right.

column. These articles were collected and published as the book *The Conscience of a Conservative*, which catapulted him to the forefront of the conservative movement.

Goldwater further earned the support of the right with his opposition to the Civil Rights Act of 1964 and by his support of an even more aggressive approach to fighting the Vietnam War. Nominated by the Republican Party as its presidential candidate in 1964, he was soundly defeated by the Democratic incumbent, Lyndon B. Johnson, carrying only his home state of Arizona and five Southern states. In the election, he found himself hurt by statements he had made, like "Extremism in the defense of liberty is no vice. And let me remind you that moderation in the pursuit of justice is no virtue."

Goldwater spent the remainder of his political career in the U.S. Senate as the grand old man of conservative politics. Paradoxically, by the 1980s, the growing influence of the Christian right on the Republican Party so conflicted with Goldwater's own libertarian views of personal liberty that he became a vocal opponent of the religious right on issues like abortion and gay rights.

Hillary heard Dr. King give a sermon entitled "Sleeping Through the Revolution." In it, Dr. King blended the message of God with the idealism of politics. "Vanity asks the question, Is it popular?" he said. "Conscience asks the question, Is it right?"[13] Hillary was becoming more and more certain how to answer the question, "Is it right?" What she had not yet resolved was what she could do to help fix what was wrong with the nation. She dreamed of becoming a doctor but was uncertain if that career could satisfy her ambitions and what she increasingly saw as her role to "do all the good you can, by all the means you can."

She was still a Republican, and as a "Goldwater Girl," worked while still in high school for her hero Barry Goldwater in the 1964 presidential elections (he lost in a landslide to Democrat Lyndon Baines Johnson). At the same time, her social concerns were leading her in the opposite direction, as the causes of civil rights and increased United States involvement in Vietnam were becoming issues for her as well as for others of her generation.

There were already many facets to her personality. She was intelligent and ambitious. She was angry at injustice and chafed at her father's restrictions. She felt a calling to social service and helping others. She had faced what she felt were humiliating defeats, yet she remained extremely confident in her own ability to overcome any obstacles put before her. She was, in many ways, a typical teenage girl of her time, yet we can already see the beginnings of the woman that she has become.

She was still just a senior in high school. Like most seniors, Hillary was facing the most important decision she would make up to that time. She knew that she was going to college but still hadn't the faintest clue as to where she wanted to go. Her decision would point her life in a direction she probably never could have dreamed possible.

Changing

Unsure where to go to college, Hillary Rodham visited her high school's college counselor, who offered her little more than a handful of brochures for Midwestern colleges but no real advice. Frustrated, she turned to two recent college graduates who were teaching government classes at her high school. The women advised her to apply to Smith or Wellesley—two of the Seven Sisters women's colleges. Their reason for recommending an all-women's college? They felt that getting an education was easier without the distraction of having men on campus and having to contend with the stereotypical role-playing of men and women. (As a fellow graduate noted in *A Woman in Charge*, "You don't have the thing where women don't put their hands up because someone might not take you out because you know the answer and they don't."[1]) At Wellesley, women were better able, as Hillary said in her autobiography, to "take risks, make mistakes, and even fail in front of one another."[2]

Although she had not considered going east for college, she was intrigued and challenged by the idea and, after getting her parents' permission, applied to and was accepted by both schools. Unable to visit the campuses personally, she made her choice based on photographs of both campuses, deciding on Wellesley because of the beauty of its Lake Waban.

For the first time in her life, Hillary Rodham, who had never even spent a weekend alone away from home, was on her own. A conservative Midwestern girl, she was now living with a largely privileged group of girls who came from money, had attended private schools, had been in the top one percent of their classes, and possessed a maturity and sophistication that Hillary still lacked. She was, as they say, playing in the big leagues.

At first, she did not like it. She felt completely out of place, struggled with her classes, and was ready to quit after one semester. Her father gave her permission to come back home, but her mother felt differently. She had not raised her daughter to be a quitter and urged her to stick it out. Hillary agreed with her mother, and as time passed, she grew to love Wellesley, a place where she could learn and be herself. What she probably did not realize was how much she, along with the rest of her class and generation, would be transformed over the next four years.

THE CHANGING TIMES

In 1994, the PBS television series *Frontline* produced a documentary about the Wellesley class of 1969, "Hillary's Class." What made the class of 1969 so interesting? As producer Rachel Dretzin said about that group of young women, "They've made a journey unlike any other generation, through a time of profound change and upheaval for women."[3] And indeed they did. It can be difficult from our vantage point to put ourselves in their shoes, to fully realize the differences in their lives between 1965 and 1969; changes that ranged from the rules of dating to the political upheaval that was soon to engulf the nation.

One major change was in their roles as women. In 1965, it was still assumed that the highest goal of a Wellesley student was to marry an Ivy League graduate and assist him in his career. It was also assumed that the school was there to protect the student—to be her parent away from home. Students had 1 A.M. curfews, and men were only allowed in the women's dorm rooms on Sundays from 2 to 5:30 P.M., and then only with the door open. Students could not drive cars on campus. They could not wear jeans or pants in the dining hall or off campus. By 1969, those rules had fallen by the wayside.

Not only were the rules governing women's behavior changing, their political beliefs were changing as well. As a freshman, Hillary had joined the Wellesley Young Republicans club and by the end of her second semester had become its president; by 1968 she was a fervent supporter of Democratic Senator Eugene McCarthy, whose opposition to the Vietnam War mirrored her own.

It had been a slow progression. Hillary had had growing doubts about the Republican Party and its policies for years, particularly regarding civil rights and the Vietnam War. Wellesley exposed her to a range of thought that was absent from Park Ridge, Illinois, and she soon found out that the ideas that she came to college with were no longer the ones she held to be true. She was aided along the way by her continuing correspondence with the Reverend Donald Jones. In one particularly poignant letter to him, she asked, "Can one be a mind conservative and a heart liberal?"[4] Although she still did not consider herself a Democrat,

Hillary Rodham is seen in a photograph taken during her student days at Wellesley College in Massachusetts. Her years
at Wellesley, from 1965 to 1969, came during a time when
women's roles were drastically changing and the nation was
deeply divided by protests and political upheaval.

before long, she had resigned as president of the Young Republicans. She now considered herself "a progressive, an ethical Christian, and a political activist."[5]

The 1960s was, of course, a time *of* political activism. Students constantly thought, talked, and argued over the nation's problems and what could be done to solve them. The war in Vietnam was at the center of most conversations. The draft was still in effect, and although women were not eligible, everybody at Wellesley knew somebody who was facing the possibility of getting drafted and sent to fight in Vietnam. Student protests against what they and many others saw as an unjust war grew, as everyone was forced to take sides for or against the war.

For Hillary, then a college junior, 1968 was the tipping point. The Tet offensive turned more and more Americans against the Vietnam War. President Lyndon Johnson, facing strong anti-war opposition from within his own party, announced that he would not seek re-election. On April 4, Dr. Martin Luther King, Jr., was assassinated, and many American cities erupted in riots. College campuses saw a new wave of protests as well, and on many campuses students took over buildings demanding, among other things, an end to the war. On June 5, Senator Robert F. Kennedy, brother of the assassinated U.S. President John F. Kennedy, and an anti-war candidate for the presidency, was himself assassinated in Los Angeles, California. To many Americans, it seemed as though the country was beginning to fall apart.

Hillary Rodham, while opposed to the war, was against the violent demonstrations that were becoming all too common. A strong believer in the law, she saw the need to work *within* the system, rather than protest from outside. Hillary had spent her years at Wellesley becoming part of that system, slowly working her way up the school's political ladder. As a sophomore she was a class representative to the student senate. The next year, she was chosen as chairman of the "Vil Juniors"—the group selected for their maturity and sense of responsibility to counsel incoming freshmen. And in February 1968, after a rigorous three-week campaign during which she outworked and out-organized her opponents, she was elected student body president. Instead of joining the protesters, she saw her role as one of using her political influence to mediate between the school administration and the angry students.

A case in point was the assassination of Dr. King. Since meeting him in Chicago, he had been one of her heroes, and for her his death was a personal loss. When Hillary heard the news of his assassination, she raced into a friend's dorm room and threw her book bag against the wall, screaming, according to a witness, "I can't stand it anymore! I can't take it!"[6] The following day, she joined in a march of protest and mourning in Boston, returning to campus wearing a black armband symbolizing her grief. But in the aftermath of the assassination, when students threatened to go on a hunger strike or even close down the campus if Wellesley did not meet their demands to recruit more black faculty members and students, Hillary stepped in.

Working as a go-between among students, faculty, and the college administration, she was able to help bring about a compromise. The students stepped back from their threats to shut down the campus, and the school initiated policies to increase recruitment of black students and faculty.

Not content to be involved solely in campus politics, Hillary also spent weekends going up to New Hampshire to stuff envelopes and campaign for Democratic anti-war presidential candidate Eugene McCarthy. Her work there, and the opportunity to meet the candidate himself, pushed Hillary even further from her father's Republican Party and toward the Democrats.

It was somewhat surprising then that, for her spot in Wellesley's Washington Internship Program, which placed students in agencies and congressional offices for a nine-week summer program, she was assigned to intern at the House Republican Conference. Hillary protested, but the program's director, who knew that she was moving away from her earlier Republican beliefs, felt that the program would help her toward making her final decision, no matter what it was. So it was that in the summer of 1968, Hillary found herself reporting to a group headed by then House Minority Leader Gerald Ford and Representatives Melvin Laird and Charles Goodell.

Like most interns, her time was largely spent answering phones and delivering messages, but she did manage to make a strong impression on her employers and was not afraid to let her opposition to the war be known. Laird, who became secretary of defense under President Richard Nixon, said in *A Woman in Charge* that "she presented her viewpoints very forcibly, always had ideas, always defended what she had in mind."[7]

Her internship with the House Republican Conference did leave her with one treasured memento—a photograph taken of her with her three advisers. This picture of Hillary alongside the Republican leadership of the U.S. House of Representatives made her father very proud, and it was still hanging on his bedroom wall when he died in 1993.

Toward the end of her internship, Congressman Goodell asked Hillary and a few other interns to accompany him to the Republican National Convention in Miami, Florida. Hillary, in theory still a Republican, was eager to go with him to try to help Governor Nelson Rockefeller of New York stop Richard Nixon from becoming the Republican nominee. It was an impossible quest: Nixon became the nominee, cementing the ascension of the conservative branch of the party over its more liberal branch, headed by Rockefeller. It was this triumph of the conservatives that finally forced Hillary and many like her out of the Republican Party. As she mused in her autobiography, "I sometimes think that I didn't leave the Republican Party as much as it left me."[8]

Hillary had changed a great deal from the girl who had gone to Wellesley just three years earlier. No longer a committed Republican, she was now a stalwart opponent of the Vietnam War. Gone too was the flipped hair and matching sweater sets, replaced by torn, faded blue jeans and long, frizzy, unkempt hair. The one-time Goldwater Girl had transformed herself into a '60s political activist.

Returning to Wellesley for her senior year, she began her thesis, analyzing the work of a Chicago community organizer named Saul Alinsky. Alinsky believed that social change began on the bottom, with grass-roots organizations that taught people how to confront government to obtain their demands. Although Hillary believed in people empowering themselves, she disagreed with Alinsky's basic premise that you could only change the system from the outside. She believed (and still does) that

IN HER OWN WORDS

About her political transition, which took place during the 1960s, Hillary Clinton would later say, as cited on About.com:

> I have gone from a Barry Goldwater Republican to a New Democrat, but I think my underlying values have remained consistent: individual responsibility and community. I do not see those as being mutually inconsistent.

it takes working from within the government to bring about change.

It was this belief that led to her decision to go to law school after graduation. By studying law, she felt that she would be better equipped to help bring about the changes needed to end the war and improve people's lives. She applied to several schools and was accepted by Harvard and Yale, two of the nation's finest. Unable to make up her mind which to attend, she made her decision when a male law school student introduced her to a famous Harvard law professor, saying, "This is Hillary Rodham. She's trying to decide whether to come here next year or sign up with our closest competitor." As Hillary describes the scene in her autobiography, the professor looked her up and down and said, "Well, first of all, we don't have any close competitors. Secondly, we don't need any more women at Harvard."[9] The decision was made for her—she was going to Yale.

(It is interesting to consider here the strange ways in which history is made. If she had gone to Harvard instead of Yale, it seems likely that she would never have met Bill Clinton. If the two had not met, would he have become president without her influence and support? In what direction would her career have gone?)

THE SPEECH

With graduation approaching, an opportunity arose for Hillary to make her first mark on the national stage. Wellesley had never had a student speaker at graduation, but given the political climate, many students felt that the time was right. School President Ruth Adams was pressured to allow a student speaker, and she gave in to the students' demands. The obvious choice to make a speech? Class president Hillary Rodham. Hillary was excited about the honor and spent hours talking to friends and classmates, finding out what it was they wanted her to say. Writing the speech came slowly, and it was the night before graduation when she actually wrote it, pulling her last all-nighter in college.

The official commencement speaker that day, May 31, 1969, was Senator Edward Brooke of Massachusetts, the Senate's only African-American member and a Republican whom Hillary had campaigned for while still a Young Republican. Senator Brooke used the opportunity to speak of his disapproval of the war protests and to seemingly defend the war. To Hillary and to her fellow graduates, however, what was more important was what he did not say. The senator did not acknowledge the grievances and concerns that the students had regarding the country's direction, and he failed to even mention the deaths of Dr. King and Robert F. Kennedy, two of the defining events for the class of 1969.

When Hillary stood up to make her speech, she was understandably nervous. She was suffering from a lack of sleep, and she had the added pressure of being the first student commencement speaker since the school's founding in 1875. She began by saying:

> I find myself in a familiar position, that of reacting, something that our generation has been doing for quite a while now. We're not in the positions yet of leadership and power, but we do have that indispensable task of criticizing and constructive . . . protest, and I find myself reacting just briefly to some of the things that Senator Brooke said. Part of the problem with empathy, with professed goals, is that empathy doesn't do us anything. We've had lots of empathy, we've had lots of sympathy, but we feel that for too long our leaders have used politics as the art of the possible. And the challenge now is to practice politics as the art of making what appears to be impossible, possible.[10]

In her commencement address in 1969 at Wellesley, Hillary Rodham spoke about her generation's fears and its loss of trust. Her speech earned her national attention, and she was featured in an article in *Life* magazine. Here, she talks about student protests for the article.

She went on to say that the most important part of that task was to end the war. She spoke of the need of her generation to ask questions, about Wellesley's policies, about civil rights, about women's rights, about Vietnam. She defended protests as "an attempt to forge an identity in this particular age," and as a way "of coming to terms with our human-ness."[11] She spoke of the fears that her generation had, the feeling of "exploring a world that none of us understands and attempting to create within that uncertainty."[12] She spoke of her generation's loss of trust, saying, "What can you say about a feeling that permeates a generation and that perhaps is not even understood by those who are distrusted?"[13]

At the end of the speech, she received a tumultuous standing ovation, but little did Hillary know that her speech touched a chord across the country. When she called home to speak to her mother, who had been ill and unable to attend the ceremony, she learned that reporters and television shows had been calling the house asking for interviews and appearances. She appeared on Irv Kupcinet's interview show in Chicago and was featured in an article in *Life* magazine, along with another student activist from Brown University named Ira Magaziner. (Magaziner went on to become President Bill Clinton's senior adviser for policy development, especially as chief health care policy developer.) Like it or not, Hillary Rodham had become a representative for her generation of women.

In the meantime, Hillary took the summer off before beginning law school in the fall. She worked her way across Alaska, first washing dishes at Mount McKinley National Park and then sliming fish, wearing knee-high boots and standing in bloody water while taking the guts from the salmon with a spoon. Years later, while first lady, she told an audience that "of all the jobs I've had, sliming fish was pretty good preparation for life in Washington."[14] But before that, her time at Yale Law School would bring new interests to her activism and introduce her to the man who would become her husband and, later, the forty-second president of the United States.

Law and
Bill Clinton at Yale

When Hillary Rodham arrived at Yale in the fall of 1969, she was one of just 27 women among 235 law students. (In 2007, women made up 46 percent of the Yale Law School student body.) She had already earned a name and reputation, perhaps only slightly exaggerated, for being a leader and an activist. "We were awed by her courage," classmate Carolyn Ellis said in *A Woman in Charge*. "She arrived with many of us thinking of her as a leader already. We had seen her picture in the national magazine, and here she was, three months later, in our class."[1]

Throughout her first year at Yale, political tensions continued to grow, both on campus and throughout the country. In April 1970, thousands of protesters descended upon Yale and the city of New Haven as eight members of the Black Panthers, a radical African-American civil-rights organization, were put on trial for murder. On April 30, President Richard Nixon announced that he would be sending U.S. troops into Cambodia, further expanding the already unpopular Vietnam War. On May 4, National Guard troops opened fire on unarmed students protesting the war at Kent State University in Ohio. Four students were killed. To many students, it was beginning to seem as though the government was at war with its own people, and the protests grew in intensity and in violence.

Rodham, while sympathizing with the protesters, remained convinced that violent, extreme protests were wrong. A strong believer in working within the system rather than working for disruption and "revolution," she continued to use her growing influence on campus to calm tempers and to steer the demonstrations away from violence and toward achieving realistic goals within the system.

She was making an impact outside of Yale as well. On May 7, 1970, Rodham addressed the convention banquet celebrating the fiftieth anniversary of the League of Women Voters in Washington D.C. As her generation's representative to an older generation of women, Rodham, wearing a black armband in memory of the students killed at Kent State, made her positions clear. She argued that President Nixon's expansion of the war into Cambodia was illegal and unconstitutional, and she tried to explain the impact that the war and Kent State had had on her class and why the protests were taking place.

The keynote speaker at the convention was Marian Wright Edelman, one of Rodham's heroes for her efforts to *use* the system, largely the courts, to work on behalf of children. Her work inspired Rodham to become an advocate for children's rights, and when Edelman had spoken at Yale in early 1970, Rodham used the opportunity to introduce herself and to ask for a summer job. Edelman told Rodham that she would be happy to hire her, but had no money to pay her. Not willing to take no for an answer (and not in a position to work for free), Rodham persuaded the Law Students Civil Rights Research Council to give her a grant, allowing her to spend the summer in Washington, D.C., working for Edelman.

The Senate was holding hearings that summer to investigate the harsh living and working conditions of migrant farm workers, and Edelman assigned Rodham to do research on the education and health of migrant children. Rodham had some firsthand knowledge of the subject, having baby-sat children in migrant camps in Illinois in a program set up by her Sunday school. She was eager to learn more, and by the time the summer program had ended, Rodham was determined to concentrate her studies on how the law affected children.

Returning to Yale in the fall of 1970, Rodham began to study child development at the Yale Child Study Center. She also began to work for the New Haven Legal Services office, where she learned the importance of children having their own advocates in situations involving abuse and neglect. In one case, Rodham assisted attorney Penn Rhodeen in representing an African-American woman who had served as a foster mother for a two-year-old girl since the girl's birth. This woman had raised children of her own and now wanted to adopt the little girl.

The Connecticut Department of Social Services, however, had a policy that foster parents were not eligible to adopt and so removed the child from the woman's home and placed her with what it saw as a more "suitable" family. Rhodeen sued the government, arguing that the foster mother was the only parent the little girl had ever known and that taking her away from that parent would do the child long-lasting harm. They lost the case, but as Clinton said in her autobiography, "It spurred me to look for ways that children's developmental needs and rights could be recognized within the legal system. I realized that what I wanted to do with the law was to give voice to children who were not being heard."[2] That fall, besides discovering where her interest in law lay, she also met the man who would force her to reconsider her own goals and dreams—Bill Clinton.

WILLIAM JEFFERSON CLINTON

Hillary Rodham had had boyfriends at Wellesley, relationships serious enough that she had taken the men home to Illinois to meet her parents. Right from the start, though, her relationship with Bill Clinton was different. A native of Arkansas, Clinton had attended Georgetown University and then Oxford University as a Rhodes Scholar before entering Yale Law School. As Hillary described him in her autobiography:

> He arrived at Yale Law School looking more like a Viking than a Rhodes Scholar returning from two years at Oxford. He was tall and handsome somewhere beneath that reddish brown beard and curly mane of hair. He also had a vitality that seemed to shoot out of his pores.[3]

Bill Clinton, too, had taken notice of Hillary Rodham, saying in his own autobiography that:

> One day, when I was sitting in the back of Professor Emerson's class, I spotted a woman I hadn't seen before. . . . She had thick dark blond hair and wore eyeglasses and no makeup, but she conveyed a sense of strength and self-possession I had rarely seen in anyone, man or woman.[4]

The two would see each other around campus, but it wasn't until the spring of 1971 that they actually met. She was studying in the library when she saw Clinton standing in the hallway, supposedly chatting with a fellow student but continuously looking over at her. Boldly for a young woman of that time, she got up from her desk, went over to Clinton, and introduced herself, saying, "If you're going to keep looking at me, and I'm going to keep looking back, we might as well be introduced. I'm Hillary Rodham."[5] When Bill Clinton tells the story, he admits to being unable to remember his own name.

The two did not speak again until the last day of classes that spring. The pair walked out of their political and civil rights course at the same time, and Clinton asked her where she was going. Rodham said she was going to the registrar's office to sign up for the next semester's classes. Clinton said he was going there as well and walked her over. While the two waited in line, they chatted, Clinton asking her about her family and where she grew up. When they got to the head of the line, the registrar looked up at Clinton and said, "Bill, what are you doing here? You've already registered!"[6] He was forced to admit that he had just wanted to spend time with her, and the pair went for a long walk that turned into their first date.

They talked for hours as they viewed an exhibit of the artist Mark Rothko at the Yale Art Gallery, and Rodham was so impressed by Clinton's wide range of interests that she impulsively invited him to a party that her room-mate, Kwan Kwan Tan, was throwing that night. Clinton remained silent throughout the party, though, and Rodham, not sure if he was shy or just uncomfortable, decided that they did not have much hope as a couple.

Besides, she already had a boyfriend and had plans to spend that weekend out of town with him. When she returned to school Sunday evening, Clinton called her up, heard her coughing from a cold she had picked up, and arrived at her house 30 minutes later with chicken soup and orange juice. As the two started to talk, she asked him why he had hardly said a word at the party. "Because I was interested in learning more about you and your friends," he replied.[7] Soon after, the two were inseparable.

They seemed made for each other. Both were smart and ambitious, both believed in the importance of public service, and both cared deeply about civil rights, ending the war in Vietnam, and a wide range of other issues. A mutual friend, Deborah Sale, described the pair in *A Woman in Charge*:

> Their values are the same. Their ambitions are the same. The passions that they have in life are the same. The kind of engagement they have, intellectual and otherwise, is really something. And to my mind they were a perfectly reasonable couple.[8]

For Hillary Rodham, Bill Clinton was perhaps the first man she had known who could stand up to her on every level, who could both challenge her and inspire her; the first man, perhaps, who wasn't afraid of her. For Bill Clinton, Hillary Rodham was like nobody he had ever met before, smart, attractive and ambitious, and independent enough to make Clinton think that she really did not need him. It was an ideal match.

Many years later, Hillary Clinton was asked to name her most ecstatic memory of her twenties. Without a moment's thought, she answered, "Falling in love with Bill Clinton."[9] One passage in her autobiography, *Living History*, shows the depth of her feelings:

> To this day, he can astonish me with the connections he weaves between ideas and words and how he makes it all sound like music. I still love the way he thinks and the way he looks. One of the first things I noticed about Bill was the shape of his hands. His wrists are narrow and his fingers tapered and deft,

like those of a pianist or a surgeon. When we first
met as students, I loved watching him turn the pages
of a book.[10]

As the spring semester of 1971 came to a close, Bill
Clinton and Hillary Rodham had many long conversations
about their futures. Rodham knew that she was interested
in child advocacy and civil rights but was unsure how to
turn that into a career. Clinton was certain of his path: He
was going to return home to Arkansas and run for public office. For the time being, though, there were more
immediate plans.

Rodham had plans to work as a summer clerk at a law
firm in Oakland, California. Clinton had already signed
up to work on Senator George McGovern's presidential
campaign as an organizer in the South. It would be a great
opportunity for him, giving him his first chance to be in
on the ground floor of a presidential campaign. Much to
Rodham's surprise, he told her that he would rather go
to California with her. He had found her, he said, they
were destined to be together, and he did not want to take
a chance on losing her. "I just liked . . . being around her,
because I thought I'd never be bored with her," Clinton said
in his autobiography. "In the beginning, I used to tell her
that I would like being old with her. That I thought that was
an important thing."[11]

The two shared a small apartment near the campus
of the University of California at Berkeley. While she
spent her time doing research and writing legal motions
and briefs for a child custody case, he explored Berkeley,
Oakland, and San Francisco. On weekends, he would take
her to the places he had discovered. They would go on long
walks, play tennis, and talk about the books that Clinton
was reading.

By the time they returned to New Haven, it was obvious that they were going to live together. They rented a small apartment for $75 a month that Rodham loved, even though "the floors were so uneven that plates would slide off the dining table if we didn't keep little wooden blocks under the table legs to level them. The wind howled through cracks in the walls that we stuffed with newspapers."[12]

The couple took yoga classes at the local Y, went to movies, and ate at their favorite inexpensive restaurants. They also made time to stay involved in politics. Clinton had opened a George McGovern for President headquarters in New Haven, using his own money to rent a storefront. The two believed strongly that McGovern was the only candidate who would bring American troops home from Vietnam, and, using a combination of persuasion and organizational strength, they prodded the local Democratic organization to endorse their candidate.

Over the Christmas holidays that year, Clinton drove from his mother's home in Hot Springs, Arkansas, to spend time with Rodham and her family. It was the first time he would be spending any length of time with her parents, and Rodham was nervous. Hugh Rodham was naturally critical of any of her boyfriends—who could possibly be good enough for his only daughter? "I wondered what he could say to a Southern Democrat with Elvis sideburns," she recalled in her autobiography.[13] As it turned out, there was little need to worry. Clinton quickly won over Hillary's mother with his good manners and willingness to help with the dishes. But what really sealed the deal was when he found Dorothy reading a philosophy book for a college class she was taking and spent the next hour discussing it with her.

Her father, naturally, took longer to accept his daughter's new boyfriend. Even he finally succumbed to Clinton's charm over numerous games of cards and time spent in front of the television watching football. Hillary's friends approved of Bill as well. Even her friend Betsy Johnson's mother approved, telling Hillary, "I don't care what you do, but don't let this one go. He's the only one I've ever seen make you laugh!"[14] When school ended in the spring of 1972, Rodham returned to Washington to work once again for Marian Wright Edelman. Clinton took a full-time position with the McGovern campaign. McGovern was poised to win the Democratic nomination for president, and Clinton was eager to do all he could to help McGovern defeat Richard Nixon in the general election.

Once McGovern won his party's nomination in Miami, Clinton was asked to help run the McGovern campaign in Texas. Clinton asked Rodham if she would like to come down as well, and she said yes, but only if she had a specific job to do. Rodham was offered the role of heading up the voter-registration drive in Texas, and she leaped at the opportunity.

MAKING CONNECTIONS

At first, she must have seemed out of place: a young blond woman from Chicago and the Northeast, who did not speak a word of Spanish, going door to door through some of the state's toughest areas to register voters for McGovern. Her tenacity and dedication made an impression on nearly everybody she worked with. Sara Ehrman, a fellow McGovern worker with whom she shared an apartment in San Antonio, called Rodham "fearless," and described her in *A Woman in Charge* as someone who "came into campaign headquarters a kid—in brown corduroy pants, brown shirt, brown hair, brown glasses, no makeup, brown shoes. Her Coke-bottle glasses. Long hair. She looked like the campus intellectual that she was. She totally disregarded her appearance."[15]

Ehrman discovered that Rodham, despite her appearance, seemed almost driven to do good. "I'd call it a kind of fervor, and self-justification that God is on her side," she remembered in *A Woman in Charge*.[16] She went on to describe the Hillary Rodham that she knew as a "progressive Christian in that she believed in litigation to do good, and to correct injustices and to live by a kind of spiritual high-mindedness."[17] According to Ehrman, Rodham carried her Bible with her everywhere she went, marking in it and carefully underlining as she read.

Most people who met Rodham saw her as intelligent and driven, but as somewhat reserved and serious. It was Bill Clinton who was able to bring out other sides of her personality—sides that she tended to keep hidden from view. "Bill Clinton tapped into part of Hillary that no one ever had," Ehrman said. "He saw the side of her that liked spontaneity and laughter. He found her guttural laugh: it's fabulous—there's nothing held back. The public never sees that side of her. When she's laughing, that's when she's free."[18] One of the people whom Rodham most impressed was Betsey Wright, a longtime political worker who was a mentor for many young women interested in politics. Wright grew close to both Bill and Hillary, but told Bill Clinton biographer David Maraniss that initially "I was less interested in Bill's political future than Hillary's. I was obsessed with how far Hillary might go, with her mixture of brilliance, ambition, and self-assuredness. There was an assumption about all the incredible things she could do in the world."[19] McGovern went on to lose the election in a landslide to Nixon. Despite the loss, Rodham's time in Texas had been invaluable. She had made an important political ally in Wright, and many of the Texans she met in 1972 would become a vital part of the political network she used to win the Texas presidential primary in 2008.

But that was many years in the future. When Rodham and Clinton graduated Yale in the spring of 1973 (she had made her first sacrifice for him by staying at Yale an extra year rather than graduating with her own class), they celebrated by going to Europe to revisit Bill's favorite places from when he was there as a Rhodes Scholar. While in the Lake District of England, Bill Clinton asked Hillary Rodham to marry him. Sure that she was in love with him, but still unsure about her own life and future, she told him, "No, not now," meaning that she was not ready. Clinton understood and asked her to marry him on many other occasions. She always said no. Eventually, according to her autobiography, he said, "Well, I'm not going to ask you to marry me anymore, and if you ever decide you want to marry me than you have to tell me."[20] Clinton knew that Rodham was the woman he wanted, and he was determined to wait as long as necessary for her to come around.

WASHINGTON OR ARKANSAS?

Coming back from Europe in the fall of 1973, Hillary Rodham had important decisions to make. Bill Clinton was returning to Arkansas to take a teaching position at the University of Arkansas School of Law in Fayetteville. She was moving to Cambridge, Massachusetts, where she went to work for Marian Wright Edelman's new organization, the Children's Defense Fund. Rodham loved the work, which involved travel and exposure to the problems affecting children and teenagers nationwide.

In South Carolina, for example, she investigated prison conditions for juveniles being held in adult jails. In New Bedford, Massachusetts, she went door to door trying to discover why some students were not attending school. She found that the children weren't in school because of physical disabilities, such as blindness and deafness, or because they were wheelchair-bound and unable to get to school.

In both of these cases, the Children's Defense Fund brought about badly needed changes. In South Carolina, the group led an effort to separate juveniles from the adult prisoners and to provide them with protection. And two years later, due in no small part to urging from the Children's Defense Fund, Congress passed the Education for All Handicapped Children Act, mandating that children with physical, emotional, and learning disabilities must be educated in the public-school system.

Rodham found the work deeply satisfying, but she was lonely in Massachusetts (it was the first time in her life that she had lived alone) and missed Clinton. That summer, she had taken the Arkansas and Washington, D.C., bar exams (the tests that determine whether a person is qualified to practice law in a given state). She easily passed the Arkansas exam, but much to her surprise, failed the exam in Washington. It was, perhaps, the first real "failure" of her life—and one that she kept secret for nearly 30 years. She said this about her failure in her autobiography, "When I learned that I had passed in Arkansas but failed in D.C., I thought maybe my test scores were telling me something."[21] According to friends, it seems likely that the exam must have severely shaken her self-confidence.

Clinton came up to Massachusetts to visit her on Thanksgiving in 1973. The two spent hours walking around Boston, talking about their future. He enjoyed teaching and living in Fayetteville but was considering a run for Congress. The investigation into Watergate was beginning, and Clinton felt that the Republican Party would be hurt by the scandal, making it easier for a Democrat to win against the incumbent Republican. Rodham was uncertain about what his plans meant for their future, while he recognized that if she went to Arkansas to be with him, she might be giving up her *own* future.

He had the utmost respect for her, believing that, compared with others of her generation, she stood "head and shoulders above them all in political potential. She had a big brain, a good heart, better organizational skills than I did, and political skills that were nearly as good as mine; I'd just had more experience."[22] Her happiness was essential to him, and he told her that it might be best if they went their separate ways and followed their own political paths. They agreed to discuss their future further in Arkansas, when Rodham went to spend time there after Christmas.

She had only been in Fayetteville a few days when Clinton got a phone call. It was a mutual friend, John Doar, who had been selected by the House Judiciary Committee to head the impeachment inquiry of President Richard Nixon, and he wanted Clinton to help him. Clinton turned down the offer, having decided to run for Congress, so Doar offered the position to Rodham, who was already on the list of candidates for the position.

Doar warned her that the job would pay very little, the hours would be long, and most of the work would be boring and monotonous. Despite the warnings, Rodham jumped at the opportunity to be a part of history. The new position also offered a possible solution to the couple's problem. Assuming the inquiry led to impeachment by the House and subsequent trial by the Senate, the whole process would take about a year. If Clinton won election to Congress, he would be moving to Washington in January 1975, right around the time the Nixon impeachment would be over. The couple could pursue their careers in Washington.

Rodham was one of just three women joining an elite team of 44 staff attorneys. The group worked seven days a week, often for 20 hours a day, and the work was far from exciting or glamorous. Her first assignment was to research the history and legal rules governing American impeachment cases; following that, she wrote an extensive memo summarizing her conclusions as to what did—and did not—make up an impeachable offense.

She moved on to help draft the procedural rules that the House Judiciary Committee and the House would use in the impeachment proceedings and was then assigned the task of putting together an internal memo that made clear the organization of Nixon's White House. Slowly but surely, Doar and his team put together the evidence to make a compelling case for the impeachment of President Nixon. On July 19, 1974, Doar presented the proposed articles of impeachment that specified the charges against Nixon. The House Judiciary Committee approved three articles of impeachment, including abuse of justice, obstruction of justice, and contempt of Congress.

THE WATERGATE SCANDAL

Watergate is used as a general term for a series of political scandals that took place during the presidency of Richard Nixon. What began with five men being arrested after breaking into the offices of the Democratic National Committee at the Watergate hotel complex in Washington, D.C., on June 17, 1972, soon became a scandal that reached to the top levels of the American government. The burglars were directly or indirectly employed by Nixon's Committee to Re-Elect the President.

Investigations conducted by the FBI, the Senate Watergate Committee, the House Judiciary Committee, and the press revealed that the burglary was just one of many illegal activities authorized and carried out by Nixon's staff. These activities included campaign fraud, political espionage and sabotage, illegal break-ins, illegal wiretapping, and the use of a secret slush fund to pay those who conducted the operations. This secret

Knowing that he had lost the support of Congress, Nixon resigned the presidency on August 9, 1974. While a victory for the Constitution and system of justice, it also forced Hillary Rodham into making a decision she had long delayed. She was now out of a job and uncertain of her future, both in terms of her career as well as her personal life with Bill Clinton.

The two were already intertwined politically. Clinton had declared his candidacy for Congress on February 25, 1974, and Rodham was on the phone with him and his campaign manager almost daily, giving them her advice and insights. Her friend and adviser Betsey Wright was

fund was also used as hush money to buy the silence of the men who were indicted for the June 17 break-in.

President Nixon and his staff began to conspire to cover up the break-in as early as six days after it occurred. After two years of investigations, it was revealed that Nixon had a tape recorder in his office that he used to secretly record many conversations. The battle for these tapes, which provided undeniable evidence that he had obstructed justice and tried to cover up the Watergate break-in, went all the way to the Supreme Court, which voted unanimously that the president must hand over the tapes to investigators. Sixteen days later, on August 9, 1974, faced with the certainty of an impeachment in the U.S. House of Representatives and of a conviction in the Senate, Nixon resigned, becoming the only U.S. president to have resigned from office.

John Doar *(standing, left)*, who headed the inquiry into the impeachment of Richard Nixon, and Hillary Rodham bring the impeachment charges into the House Judiciary Committee hearing room in 1974. Rodham was one of only three women among the staff of 44 attorneys on the impeachment team.

commuting on weekends from Washington to help Clinton, and even Hillary's father, Hugh, and her brother Tony spent part of the summer in Fayetteville lending a hand.

Now Rodham had to decide for herself whether she should join forces with Clinton in Arkansas. There were obvious reasons for her to do so. She had a job waiting for her in Fayetteville: assistant professor at the law school. And most important, the love of her life was there, running for Congress and relying heavily on her advice and support.

On the other hand, she was now in an enviable position regarding her own career. As Carl Bernstein points out in *A Woman in Charge*, Rodham had studied the law and how it affected both the richest and the poorest in the United

States. She had worked for one of the nation's leading advocates for children's rights. She had been an intern for the House Republican Conference. She had been a lawyer in the congressional impeachment investigation of Richard Nixon, a position that placed her "at the top of the heap of America's young public-minded lawyers."[23] Joining a top law firm in Washington or New York seemed the next logical step in what promised to be an extraordinary career.

Instead, on the same day that Nixon resigned, Hillary Rodham accepted the job she had been offered at the University of Arkansas Law School and told Bill Clinton that she would move to Fayetteville. Most of her friends were appalled. According to Rodham, her friend Sara Ehrman confronted her, asking, "Are you out of your mind? Why on earth would you throw away your future?"[24]

Despite her misgivings, Ehrman was the one who drove Rodham down to Arkansas, her belongings crammed into Erhman's Volkswagen, her bike strapped to the roof. As they made their way to Fayetteville, Ehrman continually asked her if she knew what she was doing in making the move. Her response? "No, but I'm going anyway."[25] Years later, Hillary Clinton is quoted as saying in *A Woman in Charge*, "My friends and family thought I had lost my mind. I was a little bit concerned about that as well."[26]

It was clear to both Bill Clinton and Hillary Rodham that, if they were going to survive as a couple, they would have to live in the same place. One of them would have to make career compromises, and with Clinton already running for Congress, it was up to Rodham to make the sacrifice. She would give Arkansas and her relationship with Bill Clinton a chance.

Life in Arkansas

Hillary Rodham plunged immediately into her new life in Arkansas. Her first night there, she heard her boyfriend give a campaign speech in the town square of Bentonville. The next day, she attended a reception for new law school faculty members and learned her assignments: teaching criminal law and trial advocacy, and running the legal-aid clinic and prison projects. These last two assignments made her the supervisor of the students providing legal assistance to the poor and the incarcerated. And, of course, she would be doing her part to help Bill Clinton win election to Congress.

She had never taught law school before, and at just 27 years old, was barely older than most of her students. She was one of only two women on the faculty. But she quickly settled into life on campus and life in a small Southern town, a town where everybody knew everybody—a life different from any she had ever known.

Somewhat to her surprise, she discovered that she truly enjoyed teaching. She was considered a tough teacher, especially in comparison with Bill Clinton, who was by all accounts the easiest grader in law school. If you were in Hillary Rodham's class, you needed to be thoroughly prepared, because as a student said, "If you were unprepared, she would rip you up pretty good, but not in an unfair way. She made you think, she challenged you. If she asked you a question about a case, and you gave an answer, well then—here comes another question."[1]

THEIR FIRST ELECTION

While they were both teaching law school, Clinton was also running for Congress with Rodham's full help and support. He had won the Democratic primary, and although a political newcomer, found himself running an unexpectedly close race against incumbent Republican John Paul Hammerschmidt. Rodham involved herself fully in Clinton's campaign, sometimes to the dismay of his campaign managers, who often found themselves at odds with what she felt the strategy should be.

As the campaign drew to its closing days, Clinton often found himself caught in the middle between his girlfriend's views and those of his campaign manager. The campaign needed additional funds and had been offered $15,000 from a lawyer who represented state dairy interests, with the stipulation that the money be used in Sebastian County, where it was assumed that it would be used to buy votes. Rodham adamantly opposed such a move, while Clinton's campaign managers, accustomed to the rough-and-tumble world of Arkansas politics, advised him to take advantage of the offer, even if it meant that he would have to repay the dairy interests with political favors.

Clinton sided with Rodham, and the money was not accepted. On election night, as the votes came in, he was running ahead of his opponent, with only the votes from Sebastian County still to be counted. To no one's great surprise, Hammerschmidt pulled ahead of Clinton, winning re-election to a fourth term by just 6,000 votes. Clinton's campaign deputy Paul Fray claimed that it was Rodham's ethics that kept Clinton out of Congress.

It was her first up-close view of political reality, and, according to Carl Bernstein, she learned her lessons well. She became less concerned with keeping to the high road and more concerned with results. The loss also forced her once again to re-evaluate her decision to move to Arkansas. With the loss, it was now apparent that the next office Clinton would seek would be on the state level. Staying with him would mean committing to living in Arkansas for a longer period of time than she had anticipated.

Could she be happy as the wife of a local politician? What would her role be? How would she be able to satisfy her own ambitions? While it was true that Arkansas had plenty of issues that Rodham could tackle, especially the poor state of public education, would it be enough for her?

Pondering these questions at the end of the school year, she decided to take a trip to Chicago and the East Coast to visit friends and family as well as to evaluate potential job offers and consider her future. Clinton drove her to the airport, and on the way there, they passed a red brick house with a "For Sale" sign in front of it, which Rodham casually mentioned was a sweet-looking house. When she returned from her trip, Clinton picked her up at the airport, and according to her autobiography, asked, "Do you remember that house you liked? Well, I bought it, so now you'd better marry me because I can't live in it by myself."[2]

Luckily, the three weeks away from Arkansas had convinced her that she wanted to be in Arkansas with Bill Clinton. So after saying "no" to countless marriage proposals, she finally said yes. Hillary Rodham had come to believe that she could make a difference no matter where she lived. And along with becoming Clinton's wife, she would become his political partner as well. Her own political career was on hold—nearly everything she would do from here on in would be to help push his career forward.

Not interested in having a conventional wedding, the two were married in the living room of their new house on October 11, 1975. Rodham wore a Victorian-lace-style dress that she had only purchased the day before the wedding. And once again bucking the conventions of the time, Rodham made it known that she would keep her own name. Although she was marrying Bill Clinton, she would still be Hillary Rodham. To her, her name *was* her identity, and keeping it was a way of remaining her own person, despite becoming a political wife. This decision to keep her own name, common and unsurprising today, would cause shock waves throughout the world of Arkansas politics for years to come.

NEW ELECTIONS AND A MOVE

Clinton moved quickly to restart his political career, entering the race for Arkansas state attorney general in 1976. While he traveled the state to campaign, Rodham remained in Fayetteville teaching, but she always offered advice and political counsel. Clinton won the Democratic nomination easily, virtually assuring him a victory in the general election in November. With that hurdle behind him, the Clintons went to New York City that July to attend the Democratic National Convention that would nominate Jimmy Carter as its presidential candidate.

They appeared everywhere, a young and attractive symbol of the emerging "New South." Carter, impressed, asked Bill Clinton to serve as his Arkansas state chairman and Hillary Rodham to be his field coordinator in Indiana. The position was, as Carl Bernstein pointed out, "an opportunity for Hillary to increase her own considerable political knowledge, to help raise her husband's stature in the Democratic Party (and perhaps in the next presidency) and to get herself placed on the list of the most promising prospects for appointment to presidential boards and commissions."[3] As expected, Carter won the general election against incumbent Gerald Ford, who had assumed the presidency upon the resignation of Richard Nixon. Bill Clinton also won, becoming Arkansas's attorney general, carrying 67 of the state's 75 counties.

With his victory would come changes. Hillary Rodham would have to leave Fayetteville and her teaching position to move to the state capital of Little Rock. She had grown to enjoy the small-town life and the friends she had made there, and she worried that Little Rock, the center of the state's political and business interests, might be a difficult place for her to fit in.

There was another challenge as well. Since she could no longer teach, she had to decide what she would do next. Working for any state-funded institution, or in any other public job such as prosecutor, defender, or legal-aid lawyer, might prove to be a conflict of interest with her husband's new position as attorney general. In addition, Clinton's salary was only $26,500 a year. With the couple's financial future as a priority, especially should they have children, Rodham decided that working for a private law firm might be the best solution.

Clinton recommended her to Arkansas's oldest and most prestigious law firm: the Rose Law Firm. Vince Foster, a partner at the firm and a childhood friend of Clinton's, had met Rodham the previous year and had been greatly impressed. In its entire 156-year history, the Rose

Hillary Rodham and Bill Clinton were photographed attending a church service in 1978. After moving to Arkansas in 1974, Rodham taught at the University of Arkansas Law School in Fayetteville. When Clinton was elected attorney general of Arkansas, the couple moved to the capital, Little Rock, where Rodham joined a private law firm.

Law Firm had never hired a woman, and it took a great deal of effort by Foster, and a sterling interview by Rodham, to persuade the firm's partners to hire her.

The firm offered her a new way to practice law. Her previous legal experience had been on the side of children and the underprivileged. At Rose Law Firm, she would be defending corporate interests: the firm's clients included many of Arkansas's largest and most powerful corporations, such as Tyson Foods, Wal-Mart, and Stephens Inc., the state's largest brokerage firm. The first case she handled, for example, involved a canning company that Rose was defending against a man who claimed that he had found the back half of a rat in a can of pork and beans. Although he had not eaten the rat, the man claimed that looking at it had made him so sick that he could not stop spitting, which in turn kept him from kissing his fiancée.

Even though the man sat through the trial spitting into a handkerchief, Rodham convinced the jury that the man had not really been damaged. The company argued that the rat had been thoroughly cooked in the canning process and was, in some parts of the world, considered completely edible. The jury gave the plaintiff only minimal damages, but Rodham soon came to realize that working in front of a jury was not her forte, and she shifted to non-jury work.

She enjoyed her work at the Rose Law Firm and became close friends with two of the firm's partners, Webster Hubbell and Vince Foster, who would go on to become important players in the Clintons' political life. Working for the firm also allowed her to perform "pro bono" work (services provided free of charge) in child-advocacy cases.

She also began to publish scholarly articles in the areas of children's law and family policy, including "Children's Policies: Abandonment and Neglect" in 1977 and "Children's Rights: A Legal Perspective" in 1979. Of these, an American Bar Association committee chairman later said, "Her articles were important, not because they were radically new, but because they helped formulate something that had been inchoate."[4] (Meaning that the concepts had not yet been fully developed or made whole.) And noted writer and historian Garry Wills called her "one of the more important scholar-activists of the last two decades."[5] Conservatives, though, would later try to use her theories on children's rights against her, arguing that they served to undermine the traditional rights of parents and that Rodham was dangerously anti-family.

Her interest in protecting the rights of children led her, in 1977, to co-found the Arkansas Advocates for Children and Families. This organization helped to bring about reform in Arkansas's child-welfare system and continues to advocate for children today.

That same year, President Jimmy Carter appointed her to the board of directors of the Legal Services Corporation. The board's primary responsibility was to distribute funding to the 335 local Legal Services offices around the country, all of which offered legal counsel to people who could not otherwise afford an attorney. Rodham understood full well the importance of the government providing the poor with attorneys to protect their legal rights, but many Republicans hated the idea. For the length of her term, much of which she served as chair, she fought off any attempts by Republicans to cut funding for the organization, and under her watch, the budget for the Legal Services Corporation expanded from $90 million to $300 million by the time she left the board in 1982.

FIRST LADY

In 1978, Bill Clinton faced an important political decision. He could run for governor of Arkansas with an almost certain chance of winning, or he could run for the U.S. Senate, in which case he would have to defeat the popular governor,

David Pryor, to win the Democratic nomination. Rodham leaned toward the Senate race: She relished the thought of moving to Washington and the strong possibility of getting a job working for President Carter. Polling showed that Clinton had a much better chance of winning the governor's race, and so the decision was made to stay in Arkansas.

Rodham had less involvement in Clinton's 1978 campaign for governor than in his previous races, but she was still there to critique his speeches and make certain that he was presenting himself to the public in the very best light. The Clintons were beginning to be perceived by the public as a package, and understood as a team. For some, this was a positive; others did not see it as such.

The 1978 campaign was the first in which Rodham became an issue herself, and she was subjected to public dislike and criticism as a way of attacking Clinton. Arkansas was still a very traditional state, and Clinton was often criticized for having a wife who had her own career as a lawyer and who would not even take her husband's name. "People thought his wife didn't like him enough to take his name," said one political columnist for the *Arkansas Democrat-Gazette*.[6]

Despite the criticism of his wife, Clinton easily won the Democratic nomination for governor and went on to win the general election with a resounding 63 percent of the vote, becoming the youngest governor in the country at age 31. He had captured the attention of the national media, and with Rodham as his closest adviser, the "golden couple" seemed poised for a potentially limitless political future. But because of questionable political judgment on both of their parts, the path would be far rockier than either had imagined.

GOOD TIMES AND BAD TIMES

In 1979, Rodham was made partner at the Rose Law Firm—the first female partner in the firm's history—but she did not have the time to do a lot of work at the firm. Her husband had asked her to chair the state's Rural Health Advisory Committee as part of his effort to improve access to quality health care in rural Arkansas. In this position, she successfully fought to obtain federal funds to expand medical facilities in some of Arkansas's poorest areas. She also maintained her involvement with Marian Wright Edelman and the Children's Defense Fund, which, along with her work with the Legal Services Corporation, brought her to Washington every few months.

With her own schedule and personal interests, she was not always able or willing to fulfill the traditional responsibilities of the governor's wife—attending lunches, shaking hands, and appearing at ribbon-cutting ceremonies. To many in Arkansas, she was far too "nontraditional" a first lady; too busy pursuing her own career instead of just being content to be the governor's wife.

As if her schedule wasn't busy enough, Rodham and Clinton were trying to have a baby. They had been unsuccessful for some time and began to think that it might never happen. But finally, in 1979, Rodham became pregnant. The couple was thrilled, and together they took Lamaze classes to prepare for the birth. At the time, Lamaze was a relatively new phenomenon, and very few fathers attended the birth of their children. As Hillary Clinton described it in her autobiography, she was talking with a judge and mentioned that she and her husband were attending "birthing" classes. "What?" the judge exploded. "I've always supported your husband, but I don't believe a husband has any business being there when the baby is born!"[7] Once again, Rodham's attitudes came into conflict with the more traditional attitudes of her adopted state.

She had other concerns as well about the family's financial future—the salary of a governor was not much more than that of attorney general. Knowing that her husband wasn't terribly concerned about money, she decided to take matters into her own hands, making a series of investment decisions that would haunt the Clintons for the next 20 years.

The first investment paid off nearly immediately. With the advice of a trusted friend, Jim Blair, she made a $1,000 investment in the cattle futures market. (These investments are considered highly risky, since the investors are, in essence, placing a bet on what cattle prices are going to be in the future. Three out of four investors lose money while trading in the commodities markets.) Rodham's bet paid off handsomely. Nine months after making her initial investment, she closed her account with a profit of nearly $100,000.

Her other investment did not pay off nearly as well. Another friend and adviser of the Clintons, Jim McDougal, approached them with what seemed to be a sure-fire deal. The couple would go into partnership with McDougal and his wife, Susan, to buy 230 undeveloped acres on the south bank of the White River in North Arkansas. The plan was to subdivide the property into smaller lots for vacation homes, and then sell the lots at a profit. Unfortunately, interest rates soon skyrocketed, and the market for vacation homes plummeted. The Clintons were left with a financial loss.

A BABY AND THEN DEFEAT

On February 27, 1980, the Clintons' daughter, Chelsea Victoria Clinton, was born. Hillary Rodham had to undergo a Caesarean section, but her husband still went into the operating room to witness his daughter's birth.

Rodham was determined to be the best possible mother to Chelsea. She knew that, with the very public lives that she and her husband were living, it would be essential to their daughter's well-being to protect her privacy as much as possible. In that, and in all aspects of being parents, even the Clintons' harshest critics agree that they did a splendid job raising their daughter. But as with most mothers, the first weeks and months were difficult. When it seemed impossible to get Chelsea to stop crying, Rodham would tell her, "Chelsea, this is new for both of us. I've never been a mother before and you've never been a baby. We're just going to have to help each other the best way we can."[8]

The governor was up for re-election that year as well, and the odds were stacked against him. Although he had accomplished much in his first term, voters in Arkansas seemed to be turning against him and his wife and toward the Republican nominee, Frank White. Hillary Rodham was once again an important issue in the campaign, largely because of her refusal to take her husband's last name. The Republican nominee's wife constantly referred to herself as "Mrs. Frank White," drawing a clear distinction between herself and Rodham. Even the announcement of Chelsea's birth turned out to be a political negative for the Clintons with its listing of the names "Hillary Rodham and Governor William Jefferson Clinton."

There were other issues in the election as well, including voter anger at additional taxes on car license fees that had been added to help pay for new roads that the state badly

DID YOU KNOW?

Did you know that Chelsea Clinton is named after a Joni Mitchell song? It's true. When Bill and Hillary Clinton were in London in 1978, they heard the Mitchell song "Chelsea Morning," while strolling through the neighborhood of Chelsea, and they decided then and there that should they ever have a daughter, they would name her Chelsea.

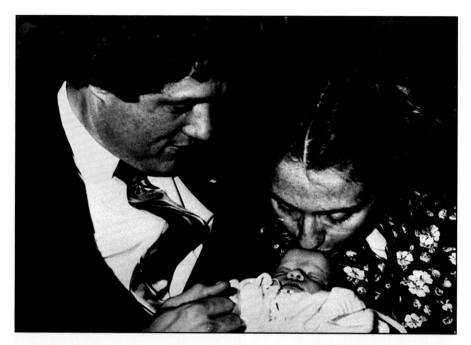

Bill Clinton and Hillary Rodham held their week-old daughter, Chelsea, for a family photo in 1980. With the two of them leading very public lives, they sought to do whatever they could to protect their daughter's privacy.

needed, and uproar at a riot by Cuban refugees who were being held by the federal government in Arkansas military camps. Rodham was the first in the campaign to believe that Clinton might lose, and she brought in pollster Dick Morris to help save the election. Despite his best efforts, Clinton lost 52 percent to 48 percent.

Naturally, Rodham was upset at the loss, but Clinton was devastated. He had now lost two out of four elections and was deeply concerned that his political career was over. Rodham knew that it was her responsibility to help her husband rebound from his loss and start to plan his next political move.

While Clinton took a position with the law firm of Wright, Lindsey & Jennings, Rodham worked to reintroduce herself to the people of Arkansas. She joined the First United Methodist Church in Little Rock and gave a series of talks around the state on why she was a Methodist. All the while, she encouraged her husband to run for governor again in 1982.

By October 1981, with the assistance of Morris and adviser Betsey Wright, who had moved to Little Rock after the 1980 election, Clinton was ready to run again. This time, Rodham was taking no chances. She would be more involved in day-to-day campaign operations then ever before and would even campaign herself, shaking hands and speaking out in defense of her husband.

It was painfully clear that, if Clinton lost this election, his political career—*their* political career—would be over. Rodham was determined that would not happen, and to help her husband win, she made changes that she had resisted for years. Gone were the long hair and informal dress: in their place were a carefully done hairstyle and conservative clothing. Rodham even did what for her had been the unthinkable: She changed her name from Hillary Rodham to Hillary Rodham Clinton, clearly signaling to conservative voters that she had listened to their concerns and had changed accordingly.

Voters responded to the new Hillary as well as to her husband's apologies for the mistakes he had made in his first term and returned him to office. Humbled by the experience, both Clintons were determined to do the job right this time. Bill Clinton decided that education reform would be the defining issue of his second term, and he placed in charge of it his closest and most trusted adviser—his wife Hillary Rodham Clinton.

She chaired the Arkansas Educational Standards Committee from 1983 to 1992, using her longstanding commitment to children's rights to help bring about badly needed changes in the state's public-education system. In what is considered one of the most important initiatives of the entire Clinton governorship, she fought a long but ultimately successful battle against the teachers union, requiring mandatory teacher testing and establishing statewide standards for curriculum and classroom size.

By doing so, Hillary played a vital role in her husband's successful bids for re-election. Education became the signature issue of his time in office. By promoting education as an idealistic cause, Hillary was able to label the opponents of her plan as "enemies" of reform, no matter what their reasons for opposition. Teachers, who opposed mandatory testing, became the opposition. When the plan became law, Governor Clinton was seen as an education reformer and as someone strong enough to stand up to the teachers union, making him virtually unbeatable.

After being re-elected in 1986 as governor to what was now a four-year term, Clinton began to receive a great deal of national attention. People began to speculate about a possible run for the White House in 1988, and neither Bill nor Hillary did anything to stop the talk. It was a serious question to consider: Was now the time to run for president?

Hillary Clinton, despite her White House ambitions, felt that the time was not right for her husband to run. And as parents, she and her husband felt that Chelsea was too young to go through the rigors of having her father running for president. Reluctantly, Bill Clinton made the announcement that he would not be running for president in 1988.

Other sources, though, say that other factors went into his decision. For many years, there had been widespread rumors that Clinton had not always been faithful to his wife. According to Carl Bernstein in his book *A Woman in Charge*, two days before his announcement, he met with Betsey Wright, who was now his chief of staff. Wright insisted that Clinton come clean with the names of any women that he might have been with, so that there would be no surprises later on. When the names were reviewed, Wright told him in no uncertain terms that it would be a political disaster for him to announce his candidacy, and it would do great harm to Chelsea and to his marriage.

After making the announcement that he would not run for president, Clinton entered another period of depression and seemed to many to be having a "mid-life crisis." At one point, he even thought of ending his marriage, but Hillary Clinton refused to consider the possibility of divorce and fought to save her marriage. The couple worked through their difficulties, and Clinton once again renewed his commitment to his wife and their family.

For a brief period, Clinton had decided not to run for re-election as governor in 1990. It was suggested that Hillary might run in his place, but polling showed that she had little chance of winning—somewhat surprisingly, she was seen as the wife of Bill Clinton, not as an individual in her own right. In the end, Clinton decided to run for re-election, and re-energized by life on the campaign trail, he won in a landslide.

Clinton's record on education, welfare reform, and economic development had earned him national acclaim, and that, along with his work with the National Governors Association, again made him a widely discussed possibility as a candidate for president. For many years, Clinton had dreamed of becoming president of the United States, and Hillary had long supported him in his quest. So once again, as the 1992 presidential elections approached, the Clintons would be facing a momentous decision: Should they take a chance and run for the White House?

Two for the Price of One

Many Democrats felt that 1992 was not going to be their year to retake the presidency. President George H.W. Bush's approval ratings remained high because of the successful outcome of the first Iraq War, and to many he seemed unbeatable. Indeed, many prominent Democrats who had considered running in 1992 ultimately decided against it. Hillary Rodham Clinton, though, had long felt that 1992 would be Bill Clinton's year to run. Her political instincts told her that Bush's popularity was not going to last, that the economy was in trouble, and that her husband could win in 1992.

The couple spent the spring and summer of 1991 discussing whether to make the run. As a politician, Bill Clinton was confident that the issues that had served him well in Arkansas—health care, education, and economic growth—were winning issues for him nationally as well. As parents, they felt that Chelsea was now old enough to understand what running for president would mean to their family. There was one major issue, however, that the couple would have to overcome if Clinton was to have any chance of becoming president—the constant rumors regarding his relationships with other women.

Bill Clinton knew whether the rumors were true or false; and while Hillary Clinton may have known or suspected the actual truth, she had made the decision to stand by her husband and fight back against any accusations of infidelity. Despite the potential difficulties, the Clintons ultimately decided that the country's needs were great, that they could make a difference, and that it was worth the risk. On October 3, 1991, with his wife and daughter by his side, Bill Clinton announced that he was running for president.

Running for national office is far different from running for statewide office, as Hillary Clinton was soon to learn. As she said in her autobiography, "Despite all the good advice we had received and all the time Bill and I had spent in the political arena, we were unprepared for the hardball politics and relentless scrutiny that comes with a run for the presidency. Bill had to make the case nationwide for his political beliefs, and we had to endure exhaustive inspection of every aspect of our lives."[1]

Hillary Clinton also learned that every comment, every statement that either of them made would be picked up by the media. Campaigning for the New Hampshire primary, the candidate introduced his wife to a crowd of supporters, telling them about her years of work on children's issues. Jokingly, he added that they had a new campaign slogan: "Buy one, get one free."[2] By saying that, he meant that Hillary Clinton would be an important part of his administration

Hillary and Bill Clinton celebrated with their daughter, Chelsea, on October 3, 1991, after Bill Clinton announced that he was running for president of the United States. Many prominent Democrats stayed out of the race, believing that President George H.W. Bush would win a second term, but Hillary Clinton felt that Bush would be vulnerable.

and would continue to champion the causes she had worked on in the past. The line took on a life of its own as it spread nationwide, and many interpreted it to mean that Hillary Clinton would be a "co-president" alongside her husband. To conservatives, the statement confirmed their long-held belief that she was overly ambitious and hungry for power. Former President Richard Nixon joined the criticism, saying that "if the wife comes through as being too strong and too intelligent, it makes the husband look like a wimp."[3] The Clintons' problems, though, were just beginning.

GENNIFER FLOWERS

On January 23, 1992, Bill Clinton, campaigning in New Hampshire, called Hillary Clinton, who was campaigning in Atlanta, Georgia, with bad news. A supermarket tabloid was about to run a story that a woman named Gennifer Flowers was claiming to have had a 12-year affair with him. He swore to his wife that the story wasn't true, and the campaign tried to ignore the tabloid reports. It quickly became apparent that the story had the potential to destroy the campaign before it had really started and that the Clintons would have to respond.

Clinton's campaign staff suggested that they both appear on the popular Sunday night television show *60 Minutes*, being broadcast that week immediately after the Super Bowl, guaranteeing a huge viewing audience. At first, Hillary Clinton strongly opposed the idea, intent on protecting her family's privacy. She soon came to realize, though, that if they did not try it, Bill Clinton's candidacy was over.

For many Americans, it was the first time they had had a serious look at the couple. Interviewed by Steve Kroft, they both declined to answer questions on whether they had ever separated or contemplated divorce, feeling that it was too much of an intrusion into their private lives. Bill Clinton did acknowledge "causing pain in my marriage" and went on to say that "you're looking at two people who love each other. This is not an arrangement or an understanding. This is a marriage."[4]

For Clinton, the appearance was enough to stop his slide in the polls. Although he only came in second place in the New Hampshire primary, he labeled himself "the comeback kid" and easily went on to win his party's nomination for president. Unfortunately for Hillary Clinton, her appearance on *60 Minutes* was the first in a series of controversial campaign moments.

In the interview, while trying to defend herself and her marriage, she said that:

> You know, I'm not sitting here, some little woman standing by my man like Tammy Wynette. I'm standing here because I love him and I respect him and I honor what he's been through and what we've been through together. And you know, if that's not enough for people, then heck, don't vote for him.[5]

In the interview, she was referring to Tammy Wynette's classic country song, "Stand by Your Man." Many took it as an attack on Wynette herself, and the reactions were loud and angry. Wynette demanded that Hillary apologize, which she did. But, as Clinton campaign adviser George Stephanopoulos noted, the interview did not fix one underlying problem: "The undercurrent we couldn't eradicate was that their partnership was less a marriage fired by love than an arrangement based on ambition."[6]

Once the fallout from the Wynette situation settled, Hillary again got herself into trouble. Questions had come up about her work with the Rose Law Firm and whether there was a conflict of interest in being a partner with a firm that did business with the state of Arkansas while her husband was governor. Asked by an NBC correspondent whether it was ethical, Hillary responded:

> You know, I suppose I could have stayed home and baked cookies and had teas, but what I decided to do was fulfill my profession, which I entered before my husband was in public life. And I've worked very, very hard to be as careful as possible, and that's all I can tell you.[7]

The media played up only the first part of her remarks, which seemed to show contempt for women who had made the decision to stay home to be wives and mothers. Once again, Hillary was forced to explain what she actually meant, and once again, she provided easy ammunition for the Clintons' political foes.

She found herself vilified by the Republican right, which saw in her everything they hated about liberals and women's rights. She was labeled "The Lady Macbeth of Arkansas" and "The Yuppie Wife from Hell."[8] She was accused of being a radical feminist who only wanted to destroy the traditional family. She was accused of being the real power behind Bill Clinton. She was accused of staying with her husband not because she loved him but because through him she could grab the power she wanted. For many, she became a symbol of all their fears and misconceptions about strong, smart, independent women.

With an election still to win, a decision was made for political partner Hillary Clinton to step back and assume the role of supportive political wife. Instead of speaking out, she would sit quietly and listen to her husband talk, applauding and waving to the crowds at the appropriate times.

The strategy worked—on November 3, 1992, Bill Clinton was elected the forty-second president of the United States. Within hours of his victory, quietly supportive political wife Hillary Clinton was gone, replaced by political partner Hillary Clinton, as the newly elected president and his first lady began to discuss who would serve in his cabinet.

WHAT WOULD HER ROLE BE?

It is known as the transition period—the frantically busy time between the election of a new president and Inauguration

Day just two and a half months later. One of the first tasks of this period is for the newly elected president to select his or her cabinet—the men and women who hold the most senior positions in the government's executive branch—positions such as secretary of state, secretary of defense, and secretary of education, as well as all other staff positions. Hillary Clinton was there every step of the way, from offering advice to actually interviewing potential candidates. To those in Washington who did not know the Clintons, her level of involvement may have been surprising; to anyone who knew them well, it was just business as usual. Deborah Sale said, "He talks to her about everything, and thinks that no one else will listen to him as carefully and challenge his ideas as constructively."[9]

One question still remained: What would Hillary Clinton's position be in the new administration? No other first lady had had a professional career upon entering the White House. And with her goals and ambitions, it was obvious that she would do more than fulfill the traditional role of first lady—but what? She, or any other member of the president's family, was prohibited by law from being a cabinet member. There was talk of her becoming the White House chief of staff. Ultimately, it was decided that her focus should be on a domestic issue—perhaps heading a task force. In the meantime, there were other things to worry about before Inauguration Day.

First, as with many other families taking a new job, the Clintons had to move all of their belongings from the Governor's Mansion to the White House. And, like any other parents, the Clintons had to find a new school for Chelsea. Bill and Hillary were determined that she should have as normal a childhood as possible. They wanted Chelsea to attend public school but ultimately decided to send her to Sidwell Friends, a private Quaker school, for one simple reason. It was a private school, so it was considered

With Hillary and Chelsea Clinton at his side, Bill Clinton was sworn in as president of the United States on January 20, 1993, in Washington, D.C. In the transition period between his election and his inauguration, many people wondered what role Hillary Clinton would play in the administration.

private property and off-limits to the news media—public schools were not. Protecting Chelsea's privacy was always their highest priority.

On January 20, 1993, as his wife and daughter held the Bible before him, William Jefferson Clinton took the oath of office to become president of the United States. A political journey that had begun years before had reached its zenith, and the first couple was about to begin an extraordinary eight years in Washington—years of political victories and years that would strain their marriage to the utmost.

It quickly became clear that Hillary Clinton was not going to be an ordinary first lady. Since the time of the

Truman administration, the first lady and her staff had their offices in the East Wing of the White House. Not Hillary. While she kept a presence in the East Wing, the Office of the First Lady was moved to the West Wing—to the very center of power, just a few feet from the Oval Office.

Some within the new administration disapproved of the new arrangements. They believed that the press, the Republicans, and the Clintons' political enemies would take advantage of any sign that the Clintons were partners in a co-presidency. Hillary Clinton fought back, arguing that

ELEANOR ROOSEVELT

Before there was Hillary Rodham Clinton, there was Eleanor Roosevelt (1884–1962), an activist and humanitarian who forever changed the role of the first lady.

The wife of President Franklin Delano Roosevelt, Eleanor Roosevelt was perhaps the most active first lady in American history. At a time when few women had careers outside the home, she traveled around the country, visiting federal relief projects, investigating working and living conditions for America's poor, and then reporting her observations back to the president. (The president, paralyzed from the waist down by polio, found it difficult to travel.) She held weekly news conferences—a first for a first lady—and she wrote her own syndicated newspaper column, "My Day."

Eleanor Roosevelt, however, was more than just the eyes and ears of the president—she had her own political and social influence. She was a tireless spokeswoman for the rights and needs of the poor, of African Americans, and of the disadvantaged. During World War II, she traveled to Europe and the her very presence in the West Wing would help symbolize to the American people the importance that her primary issues—health care and education—would have within the administration. In the end she won.

Of course, opposition to her having a West Wing office symbolized a greater source of controversy: Many critics simply felt that it was inappropriate for the first lady to play a central role in matters of public policy. Historically, the wife of the president has always been an adviser, but playing a formal role in making policy was another matter

South Pacific as a representative of her husband and to help boost the morale of U.S. servicemen and servicewomen.

After President Roosevelt's death in 1945, she remained active on a worldwide stage. She was one of the co-founders of Freedom House, an organization that advocates for democracy and human rights, and she had strongly supported the formation of the United Nations. She was a delegate to the U.N. General Assembly from 1945 to 1952, led the committee that drafted and approved the Universal Declaration of Human Rights, and was an indomitable advocate for human rights until her death in 1962. Adlai Stevenson asked at her funeral, "What other single human being has touched and transformed the existence of so many?"* Eleanor Roosevelt is one of the most admired figures of the twentieth century.

---

*John T. Marck, "Eleanor Roosevelt: First Lady of the World, Diplomat & Humanitarian," available online at http://www.aboutfamouspeople.com/article1080.html.

altogether. Hillary Clinton's supporters, though, pointed out that people were well aware when they voted for Bill Clinton that his wife would play an active role in his presidency.

Although it was expected that she would play an active role, it came as a surprise to many when, just five days after his inauguration, President Clinton appointed his wife to head the President's Task Force on National Health Care Reform. Ira Magaziner, a trusted Clinton friend and adviser who had first met Hillary Clinton in 1969 when they were both featured in *Life* magazine, would manage the day-to-day operations of the task force as a senior adviser to the president for policy and planning.

Reforming the health-care system and helping to make it affordable for all Americans was to be the centerpiece of the Clintons' first years in office. As Carl Bernstein pointed out in *A Woman in Charge*:

> The Clintons came to Washington to accomplish great things. The greatest of their goals was to establish a system of universal health care in which every American would be insured against catastrophic illness and guaranteed adequate, paid lifelong medical care. . . . "If I don't get health care done, I'll wish I didn't run for president," Bill told his aides in February.[10]

Should they achieve their goal, it would be a smashing political victory, one that would strengthen the Democratic Party for years to come and virtually guarantee his re-election in 1996. If it failed, the price could be steep. It would be up to Hillary Clinton to make it a success.

Hope and Despair

When a new president takes office, he is usually granted what is called a honeymoon period, a time when criticism is held to a minimum as he or she learns the way of office. Bill Clinton's honeymoon was a short one, cut short by errors made by both him and the first lady, with consequences that lasted for the duration of his time in office.

Hillary Clinton, committed to maintaining her and her family's privacy, ordered the corridor that had given reporters access to the West Wing closed off, infuriating members of the media whose support she badly needed. Zoë Baird, Hillary's choice to be the country's attorney general, was forced to withdraw her name from nomination after it was learned that she had broken immigration laws by hiring illegal immigrants as her chauffeur and nanny and had failed to pay Social Security taxes for them. (Clinton's second selection, Kimba Wood, was also forced to withdraw her name from nomination after it was learned that she, too, had employed illegal immigrants.) These errors in judgment, along with others, created an image of the Clintons as political amateurs who were not quite ready to play in the big leagues of Washington politics.

The Clintons received more bad news at the very beginning of Bill's term. The government's budget deficit, which President George H.W. Bush and his aides had earlier claimed was around $250 billion, was actually more than $387 billion. With that, the president's priorities shifted. Health care and all the other domestic programs that had been promised during the campaign would have to take an immediate back seat to getting a new budget and economic plan approved by Congress.

Hillary Clinton was not pleased. She feared that the fight to get the budget passed would weaken the chances for health-care reform. "We didn't come here to spend all our time cutting deficits created by Republicans," was a constant refrain.[1] The president insisted that only after the budget deficits were brought under control and the economy was moving again would new programs in health care and education be possible. (Clinton's budget plan, the Omnibus Budget Reconciliation Act of 1993, was enacted on August 8 of that year, setting the stage for a drop in the government's deficit and the growing strength of the economy throughout the 1990s.)

So while President Clinton began the fight to get his budget plan through Congress, the first lady started to work on her health-care proposal. When Clinton announced the formation of the task force, he had promised that it would produce legislation during his first 100 days in office. To most observers, this seemed an impossible goal: Such a complex piece of legislation would take a minimum of four to five years to put together and get through Congress. Hillary Clinton, though, was determined to get it passed by the mid-term elections in 1994.

Given the crisis in U.S. health care, it seemed vital to try. When President Clinton took office, nearly 37 million Americans were uninsured. (That number had jumped to 47 million by 2008.) Rising health-care costs were a burden on the economy. Doctors and hospitals raised their rates to help cover the costs of treating the uninsured, but as insurance costs increased, fewer employers were willing or able to provide coverage for their employees, leaving even more people uninsured. It was obvious that the system needed to be fixed.

Hillary Clinton herself admitted that she was not an expert on health care but was willing to immerse herself in the issue to come up with a working solution. She got off to a bad start by demanding that all meetings and deliberations be held in private and closed to the press and the public: Only after the task force had reached its final recommendations would its work become known; she felt that any advance notice of what the task force was discussing would open the floor to debate before any final decisions had been reached.

While this may have seemed like a good idea in theory, many in the media reacted to it by referring to the task force as secret or secretive, which set the stage for a backlash against the first lady long before her recommendations had been made public. Many members of Congress, Democrat and Republican alike, were upset as well, angry that they were being left out of any role in putting a bill together. It seemed to many that she was intent on alienating the very people whose support she would need to get her bill passed.

In truth, the bill, which would have required employers to provide health coverage to their employees through individual health maintenance organizations, never really had a chance. Many congressional leaders suggested that the Clintons slow the process down and wait until after the 1994 elections before trying to get the bill passed, but Hillary Clinton refused to heed their advice. Public opinion began to turn against the health-care package as well, as insurance companies, concerned that the plan would cut profits, funded a series of television ads attacking the proposed bill. Featuring a fictional couple named Harry and Louise, the ads were designed to exploit people's fears that the Clinton plan would take away their own private insurance and force them to use government insurance instead. (The proposed plan would have done no such thing.)

Still, the Clintons remained optimistic that their plan had a chance. On September 22, 1993, President Clinton gave a major address to introduce his wife's health-care plan to Congress and the nation. Over the course of his 52-minute speech, he made clear the country's need for an affordable health-care plan and carefully explained that fixing the health-care system was not just about health care alone—it also meant having a stronger economy and lower government deficits. The speech received a standing ovation, and for the first time, many Americans had a sense that the government might actually be close to providing health care to all.

Over the next few days, before the bill had even been submitted, Mrs. Clinton made the rounds of Congress, testifying before the House Ways and Means Committee, the House Energy and Commerce Committee, the Senate Labor and Human Resources Committee, the House Education and Labor Committee, and the Senate Finance Committee. No other first lady in U.S. history had been the lead witness on a major administrative initiative. Most members of those committees were dazzled by her command of the subject, her passion, and her charm. "I'm here as a mother, a wife, a daughter, a sister, a woman," she told the House Ways and Means Committee. "I'm here as an American citizen concerned about the health of her family and the health of her nation."[2]

The *New York Times* said about her testimony that:

> Hillary Rodham Clinton dazzled five Congressional committees last week, advocating health-care legislation in the most impressive testimony on as complete a program as anyone could remember, and raising hopes that an issue that has stymied Congress for fifty years was now near solution.[3]

From that high point, things quickly went downhill.

Many in Congress were astonished when details of the bill were leaked to the press before they themselves had seen them. Senator Daniel Patrick Moynihan, the powerful head of the Senate Finance Committee, called the proposed bill's financial calculations "fantasy" numbers. And when the bill finally reached Congress, it totaled 1,324 pages— not unprecedented for such a complex piece of legislation, but it made the bill an easy target of attack by the Clintons' political opponents.

The pharmaceutical and insurance industries spent millions of dollars to oppose the bill. Many Republicans as well decided to oppose the plan. William Kristol, a leading Republican strategist and commentator, sent a memo to all Republican members of Congress, urging them to kill health-care reform, calling it a "serious political threat to the Republican Party."[4] Republican ads opposing health-care reform began to be broadcast throughout the country. With the 1994 mid-term elections fast approaching, even Republicans who might have been in favor of health-care reform began to back away from the Clintons' proposal.

As opposition grew, Hillary Clinton went on a nationwide tour to speak out in favor of the plan: The tour was a

Senator Edward Kennedy, chairman of the Senate Labor and Human Resources Committee, showed Hillary Rodham Clinton to her seat prior to her testifying in September 1993 before the committee. At left was Senator Nancy Landon Kassebaum. That week, Clinton testified before five congressional committees on her health-care proposal, winning good reviews. But within a year, health-care reform was dead, with many of the wounds inflicted by Clinton herself.

disaster. Encouraged by conservative talk radio hosts, protesters showed up at every appearance, eager to voice their opposition to Hillary Clinton and her health-care plan. In Seattle the mood was so hostile that the Secret Service insisted that she wear a bulletproof vest for her own protection. Several arrests were made that day, and guns and knives were confiscated from members of the crowd.

On July 29, 1994, in an interview with the *New York Times*, Minority Whip Newt Gingrich flatly stated that House Republicans were united against health-care reform and hoped "to use the issue as a springboard to win Republican control of the House."[5] It was obvious that the issue of health-care reform was dead, at least for the time being. On September 26, 1994, Senate Majority Leader George Mitchell quietly removed the bill from consideration before it was even voted on.

What went wrong? Among the reasons were a massive advertising campaign against the bill and united opposition from leading Republicans who hoped to use the Clintons' health-care proposal as an issue to win control of Congress. Hillary Clinton had known that the battle would be a difficult one to win, but even she underestimated the fierce opposition that such a dramatic change in government policy would cause.

Clinton herself contributed to the defeat of health-care reform. The bill was perhaps overcomplicated, which made it difficult for anyone who wasn't a health-care expert to understand fully how it worked. This, in turn, made it easy to attack. Clinton also made some serious political miscalculations. The secrecy in which the initial hearings were held alienated many within the health-care industry and Congress, whose support she badly needed.

Another factor in the defeat was her complete unwillingness to compromise. She refused to accept any changes to her bill and, as in her battle for education reform in Arkansas, viewed anyone who criticized her bill as an enemy, regardless of whether they favored health-care reform or not. During this period, several other health-care initiatives were introduced in Congress by both Republicans and Democrats: If she had thrown her support behind one of those alternative bills, it seems likely that some form of health-care reform would have made it through Congress, albeit smaller in scope than Clinton's own proposals. According to U.S. Senator Bill Bradley, instead of trying to work with Congress, she threatened to "demonize" any members of Congress who tried to alter the administration's plans. To many, it was this absolute certainty that her way was the best and only way that killed any chance of health-care reform under the Clinton presidency.

SCANDALS

The proposal was also defeated for reasons outside of the issue of health-care reform itself. From its first days, the Clinton administration had found itself in the midst of one scandal after another, each of which weakened the president's political power. Often finding herself in the center of those scandals was Hillary Clinton.

The Whitewater controversy, which had first erupted during the 1992 presidential campaign, was a focus of media attention throughout Clinton's time as first lady. The Clintons *had* lost their investment in the Whitewater Development Corporation. But at the same time, their partners in that land deal, Jim and Susan McDougal, had operated Madison Guaranty, a savings and loan institution that retained the legal services of the Rose Law Firm while Clinton was a partner. The McDougals were suspected of having used Madison Guaranty to improperly subsidize Whitewater losses. So when Madison Guaranty later failed, Clinton's work at Rose came under scrutiny as investigators searched for a possible conflict of interest in representing the bank before state regulators that her husband had appointed.

At first, both Clintons failed to recognize the political significance of the interest in Whitewater. But after the *Washington Post* and the *New York Times* ran long articles, they realized that the issue was not going to go away. In November 1993, the *Washington Post* submitted a long list of questions regarding Whitewater and the McDougals to the White House, sparking a serious debate: How should the White House handle the problem?

Many of the Clintons' top political advisers recommended that they immediately turn over to the media and government investigators any and all documents regarding Whitewater. Others, led by Hillary Clinton, felt that if they were to release the documents, they would be opening themselves up to the possibility of an unending number of investigations. According to Carl Bernstein, Clinton put her foot down, saying, "These are my papers. They belong to me. I could throw them all in the Potomac River if I wanted to."[6] Hillary Clinton's refusal to allow the release of personal documents pertaining to Whitewater, combined with her stated inability to find any of her billing records for the Rose Law Firm, was all the Republicans needed to hear. They began to demand that the attorney general appoint an independent prosecutor to get to the bottom of the entire Whitewater mess. Soon, even leading Democrats such as Senator Daniel Patrick Moynihan joined the chorus for a special prosecutor, begging the White House to release all documents to stop the political damage caused by their refusal to cooperate.

Reluctantly bowing to political pressure, and against his wife's strong opposition, Bill Clinton called on his attorney general, Janet Reno, to appoint a special counsel to investigate Whitewater. On January 20, 1994, the first anniversary of the Clinton administration, Robert Fiske was named to the position, given a jurisdiction that allowed him to investigate any activity even remotely related to Whitewater.

In the midst of the Whitewater scandal, another one erupted, one whose long-term effects would ultimately lead to the president's impeachment. In December 1993, Hillary Clinton learned that the *American Spectator*, a monthly right-wing publication, was running an article about her husband's alleged sexual encounters with a large number of women while he was governor. One of the supposed encounters was with a woman referred to in the article only as "Paula." It was later revealed that her full name was Paula Jones. Jones threatened to file suit against the president in civil court unless he admitted that he had been in a hotel room with her and that no immoral conduct had occurred. Many of President Clinton's advisers and even his attorney urged him to settle the case out of court and bring it to an end. At Hillary Clinton's urging, however, he refused to admit anything, and on May 6, 1994, Jones filed a civil suit against the president, asking for $700,000 in damages.

Other problems arose as well. There was an ongoing investigation of the May 1993 firings of White House Travel Office employees, an affair that became known as "Travelgate." It was alleged that the White House had used accusations of alleged financial misconduct as an excuse to replace the travel office staff and give the White House travel business to friends from Arkansas. The subsequent investigation focused on whether Hillary Clinton herself had orchestrated the firings and whether the statements she had made regarding the firings were true.

While the final report on Travelgate found that there was substantial evidence that she was involved in the firings and that she had made "factually false" statements, there was insufficient evidence to prosecute her. There was, however, an unexpected tragedy connected to the scandal. Vince Foster, Hillary's friend and fellow attorney at Rose Law Firm, had been the deputy White House counsel. He became the subject of several hostile articles in the *Wall Street Journal* regarding his possible role in Travelgate. Suffering from clinical depression, Foster killed himself on July 20, 1993.

Hillary was devastated by her friend's suicide, but the worst was still to come. Allegations were made that she had ordered the removal of potentially damaging files (relating to Whitewater or other matters) from Foster's office on the night of his suicide. Other accusations went even further. Several right-wing organizations launched campaigns trying to prove that Foster had been murdered. One theory stated that he had been killed to stop him from revealing damaging information about the Clintons. There was no evidence to support any of these wild allegations, and to Hillary Clinton, they served as proof that the right wing was willing to say or do anything to destroy the Clinton presidency.

MID-TERM ELECTIONS

In June 1994, special counsel Robert Fiske issued his preliminary report. He found that Foster's death was suicide and not an attempt to conceal facts related to Whitewater. Fiske also found that there was no evidence that anyone in the White House had tried to influence the Madison Guaranty matter. The report seemed to vindicate the Clintons, but Republicans were not willing to accept that. They immediately attacked Fiske, complaining that he had not been truly independent, and demanded that a *new* special counsel be named.

On the same day that Fiske issued his preliminary report, President Clinton signed legislation reactivating the Office of the Independent Counsel. It was hoped that Fiske would be reappointed to allow him to complete his investigations. Republicans, though, attacked Fiske's integrity and independence, and a three-man panel named Kenneth Starr to replace Fiske. The Clintons were dismayed at the appointment, fearing that Starr, a conservative Republican, would extend the investigation for months or even years. Such an investigation could do nothing but weaken an already damaged presidency.

Despite several major successes in its first two years, by November 1994, the Clinton administration seemed to be unraveling. The investigations into Travelgate and Whitewater, along with the humiliating defeat of Hillary Clinton's health-care plan, all played a part in the dramatic shakeup of power in Washington after the November mid-term elections. The Democrats lost eight seats in the Senate and an astonishing 54 seats in the House, and for the first time since the Eisenhower administration, the Republicans controlled both the House and the Senate.

Hillary Clinton was stunned by the Democratic losses. With Congress in Republican hands, she knew that they would begin their own investigations into Whitewater, Travelgate, and whatever else they wanted. For at least the next two years, she and her husband would be under serious attack.

It had been a difficult two years for her. As Carl Bernstein noted, the cumulative effect of her father's death in 1993, Vince Foster's suicide, the ongoing Whitewater investigation, the failure of her health-care program, and the Democratic defeats in the mid-term elections was devastating to her on both a personal and a political level. She had started as first lady with such bright hopes—how could it all have gone so wrong so fast?

President Clinton was also forced to question his own actions during his first two years in office. Should he have turned health care over to his wife? Should he have ignored his own political instincts by not waiting to delay health care until after the mid-term elections? Should he have immediately turned over all papers regarding Whitewater to investigators when they were first requested? To Clinton, it must have felt that a great deal of the difficulties his administration was facing could be laid, directly or indirectly, at his wife's feet. For him to recover politically, it was clear that her role would have to change.

OUT OF THE SPOTLIGHT

For the next two years, Hillary Clinton removed herself from any leading role in policy discussion. According to Harold Ickes, the deputy White House chief of staff, "she literally withdrew. I mean, you just didn't see her. She would come over to her West Wing office from time to time. I would talk to her on the phone. But even I, who was as close to her as anybody on the president's staff, hardly saw her at all. . . . She no longer participated. . . . She didn't talk to the White House staff."[7] What had in many ways been a co-presidency was now over.

Obviously, Clinton did not stop advising her husband and did not remove herself completely from the public eye. Her role was scaled back, and she began to assume more and more of the traditional roles of the first lady. For the first time during her husband's presidency, she began to travel the world on her own, representing the United States wherever needed and speaking out on the issues that concerned her.

She visited South Asia, meeting with Prime Minister Benazir Bhutto in Pakistan and with women's groups in India, Nepal, and Bangladesh. Accompanying Clinton was daughter Chelsea, and the trip allowed them to see first-hand the incredible poverty that existed in that area of the world. The trip, though, also allowed them to see the courage of so many who were working diligently to overcome hardships and oppression.

It was a major event in her life. Journalist Joe Klein, who accompanied Clinton on the trip, said in *Time* that:

It was, I suspect, a turning point in Clinton's life. Back home she had faced dangerous, vitriol-spewing crowds at the end of the health-care battle, but each time she stepped off the big plane with the grand words "United States of America" emblazoned on its side, the crowds were huge and adoring. And as she went from place to place, visiting local programs that helped women overcome the vicious prejudices visited upon them by male-dominated cultures, a metamorphosis took place: gradually, she seemed to put the health-care debacle behind her and realize there was other work to be done, if not as co-president, then as first lady. There were all these women who needed a public voice. One day in Ahmadabad, India, she visited a remarkable economic program for untouchable women who were ragpickers. They sang "We Shall Overcome" for her in Gujarati, and tears filled her eyes.[8]

Later in the year, she visited China, as honorary chair of the U.S. delegation to the United Nations Fourth World Conference on Women. Despite concerns about negative Chinese reaction to her speech, Clinton decided, as she said in her autobiography, "to push the envelope as far as I can on behalf of women and girls."[9] Addressing the audience at Beijing's Plenary Hall, she described the women and girls she had met around the world who were working to promote education, health care, and legal rights, and to end the injustices that women suffer. She spoke out on her belief that women's rights are inseparable from human rights, saying that:

I believe that on the eve of a new millennium, it is time to break our silence. It is time for us to say here in Beijing, and the world to hear, that it is no longer acceptable to discuss women's rights as separate from human rights. . . . For too long, the history of women has been a history of silence. . . . If there is one message that echoes forth from this conference, let it be that human rights are women's rights . . . and women's rights are human rights, once and for all.[10]

The speech became, as she wrote, "a manifesto for women all over the world."[11] The *New York Times* reported on its editorial page that the speech "may have been her finest moment in public life."[12] To this day, Clinton says in her autobiography, women approach her quoting words from the speech or handing her copies to be autographed.

Upon returning from China, Clinton immersed herself in new projects. In an effort to reintroduce and humanize her to the general public, she began to write a syndicated weekly newspaper column. She also started work on a book, *It Takes a Village*.

The title of the book is taken from an African proverb: It takes a village to raise a child. This simply means that parents are not the only ones involved in raising a child. Schools, churches, neighbors, friends and family, and the community as a whole all play their parts. In the book, Clinton laid out a vision for the children of America. Everybody, she felt, from government on down, had a responsibility to ensure that children were given the love, education, and support they needed.

As 1996 began, Hillary Clinton's approval ratings with the American people had begun to rise again, and an independent report from the Resolution Trust Company (RTC) was made public, corroborating the Clintons' claim that they had had minimal involvement with the Whitewater investment and no liability in the collapse of Madison Guaranty. Unfortunately, just weeks later, as she prepared to begin a book tour to publicize *It Takes a Village*, new revelations and accusations once again put her on the defensive.

Kenneth Starr had long been requesting that Clinton turn over to him her billing records for her work with Rose Law Firm. She had long claimed, though, that the records were lost: In January 1996, though, the records suddenly turned up, found among the hundreds of boxes of files and records the Clintons had brought with them from Little Rock. Although the records ultimately revealed that Clinton's work on Whitewater had in fact been minimal, their mysterious reappearance created an impression that the first lady had not been telling the truth about the files in the first place.

The media had a field day. A *Newsweek* cover story featured the headline "Saint or Sinner" above her photo. *New York Times* columnist William Safire called her a "congenital liar."[13] And then, to make matters worse, on January 19, 1996, she received a subpoena from Starr to testify before a grand jury regarding the discovery of the billing records. It was the first time in history that a first lady had been so called. Public opinion polls taken that day showed a 10-point drop in her popularity, and a majority of Americans now thought that Clinton was a liar.

DID YOU KNOW?

Did you know that Hillary Clinton has won a Grammy Award? It's true. In 1997, she received a Grammy Award for "Best Spoken Word Album" for her recording of her book *It Takes a Village*. (Her husband won the same award in 2005 for his recording of his autobiography, *My Life*.)

Hillary Clinton was badly shaken by the turn of events. She told Barbara Walters in an interview, "You know, a month ago, people were jumping up and down because the billings were lost and they thought somebody might have destroyed them. Now the records are found and they're jumping up and down. But I'm glad the records were found. I wish they had been found a year or two ago, because they verify what I've been saying from the very beginning."[14] Despite Clinton's statements, word leaked out that Starr was considering bringing charges against the first lady.

At the same time, President Clinton's own popularity was on the upswing. By standing firm against the worst excesses of the Republican-controlled Congress, he had shown himself to be a strong and decisive leader, and his efforts regarding the economy were beginning to show results. By 1996, he had cut the nation's deficit by more than half. The economy was booming, and 10 million new jobs had been added. Taxes had been cut for 15 million low-wage workers, protections had been put in place to keep workers from losing their health-care coverage when they lost their jobs, and the minimum wage had been raised. With the successful passage of welfare reform in August 1996, President Clinton had practically assured himself re-election.

The 1996 Republican presidential nominee was Senator Bob Dole of Kansas. In his acceptance speech at the Republican National Convention, he used the opportunity to attack the first lady's book, *It Takes a Village*. Somewhat missing the point of the book, he said, "With all due respect, it does not take a village to raise a child. It takes a family to raise a child."[15]

Hillary Clinton, of course, strongly disagreed. Her argument had always been that the family was the first line of responsibility in raising a child but that society as a whole

Hillary Clinton waved as she arrived at federal court in Washington, D.C., on January 26, 1996, to testify before a grand jury. She was appearing in court to offer her explanation of why her law firm records had turned up two years after they had been subpoenaed.

shared in that responsibility. Speaking at the Democratic National Convention, where her husband was renominated, she made her response:

> For Bill and me, there has been no experience more challenging, more rewarding, and more

humbling than raising our daughter. And we have learned that to raise a happy, healthy, and hopeful child, it takes a family. It takes teachers. It takes clergy. It takes businesspeople. It takes community leaders. It takes those who protect our health and safety. It takes all of us. Yes, it takes a village. And it takes a president. It takes a president who believes not only in the potential of his own child, but of all children, who believes not only in the strength of his own family, but of the American family. It takes Bill Clinton.[16]

Bill Clinton easily won re-election, defeating Senator Dole by more than eight percentage points. He would now have the opportunity to finish the job he had started. Hillary Clinton was optimistic that the worst of the fall-out from Whitewater was behind her. She felt certain that she had learned from her mistakes, and she made plans to speak out publicly and to help shape White House policy on issues affecting women, children, and families. Little did either of them know that just two years later, the president would be impeached by the House of Representatives and fighting just to remain in office.

Tested

The next years were politically successful ones for Hillary Clinton. She continued to make overseas visits, meeting with dignitaries and speaking out on human rights. Along with Senators Ted Kennedy and Orrin Hatch, she was a force behind passage of the State Children's Health Insurance Program, a federal effort that provided state support for children whose parents were unable to provide them with health coverage. She promoted nationwide immunization against childhood illnesses and encouraged older women to seek a mammogram to detect breast cancer, with coverage provided by Medicare. She successfully worked to increase research funding for prostate cancer and childhood asthma at the National Institutes of Health.

And finally, she initiated and helped reach a compromise between Democrats and Republicans to ensure passage of the Adoption and Safe Families Act, which made it easier for foster families to adopt children with special needs. The issue had been a longtime concern of hers, and she considered the legislation her greatest accomplishment as first lady.

On a personal level, there was one traumatic change. Now a junior in high school, Chelsea Clinton had expressed an interest in attending Stanford University in Palo Alto, California. Clinton, as would most mothers, reacted badly. "What? Stanford is too far away! You can't go that far away. That's all the way over on the West Coast—three time zones away. We'd never get to see you," she remembered saying.[1]

During August 1996, mother and daughter began to tour college campuses. They started out on the East Coast, where Hillary Clinton hoped that Chelsea might want to attend her alma mater, Wellesley. It was not to be. Chelsea fell in love with Stanford at first sight and entered there as a freshman in September 1997, accompanied by her parents. Picture the scene: The president of the United States taking apart the room's bunk beds while the first lady frantically raced around trying to get her daughter's things organized and cutting up contact paper to fit the drawers. Chelsea had been the center of her parents' lives—now they were on their own.

KENNETH STARR, PAULA JONES, AND MONICA LEWINSKY

In January 1998, Kenneth Starr's inquiry was now in its fourth year, and it seemed increasingly unlikely that it would lead to any serious charges against either the president or the first lady. The Paula Jones case, though, was still pending,

The Clintons shared a laugh during convocation ceremonies in September 1997 at Stanford University in Palo Alto, California. Chelsea Clinton was entering Stanford as a freshman, and her parents were now on their own.

and within weeks the two cases would become intertwined in ways that no one could have possibly imagined. Starr had expanded his investigation into President Clinton's conduct during the sexual harassment lawsuit filed by Jones. In sworn testimony before the grand jury on January 17, 1998, Clinton had denied having a "sexual affair" with 21-year-old White House intern Monica Lewinsky. But Linda Tripp, one of Lewinsky's friends, unknown to the president and his attorneys, had provided Starr and Paula Jones's attorneys with taped phone conversations in which Lewinsky discussed having inappropriate relations with the president. Starr had the ammunition he needed to charge Clinton with perjury—making a false statement under oath.

Four days later, Hillary Clinton woke up with her husband sitting on the edge of the bed, telling her he had bad news. The *Washington Post*, he said, was publishing an article describing an affair he had with a former White House intern. Starr was now investigating whether he had lied about it under oath and whether he had asked Lewinsky to lie about it during the Jones deposition.

The president swore to his wife that the story was not true. He told her that he had been encouraging to Lewinsky when she had asked him for job advice and that she had possibly misinterpreted his willingness to help. Over and over, he insisted that nothing improper had taken place.

In her autobiography, Clinton says that she had little problem believing the new accusations were groundless. For many years, she had seen her husband attacked by political enemies, and she saw this as just one more example of an enemy willing to do or say anything to hurt him politically. She made the decision to accept his word, she said, and to stand by him politically.

There are others, though, who doubt if this was the case. Hillary Clinton knew that the president had not always been faithful to her during their marriage. Did she ever doubt him? Did she ever suspect that he did have a relationship with Lewinsky? There are friends of hers who insist that Clinton suspected that there was truth to the story; he had been unfaithful too many times in the past for her not to believe that it could have happened again.

STANDING BY HER MAN

For the Clintons, it was obvious that his presidency was in grave danger. Washington was abuzz with speculation, gossip, and discussion of how long it would be before the president was forced to resign. On ABC's *This Week*, Sam Donaldson said that it was far from certain that he would even be able to survive through the next week. It was in this charged atmosphere that Hillary Clinton took control of her husband's political survival.

Of course, for her, there was more at stake than just the president's political future: Her own was in peril as well. As her friend and adviser Sidney Blumenthal observed in the Hillary Clinton biography *Her Way*: "For her, the stakes were greater than for anyone. They encompassed not only everything they had worked on politically for a lifetime, but her marriage. She had to defend both."[2]

She immediately went on the offensive. That very same afternoon she learned about the Lewinsky accusations, she met a crowd of reporters, one of whom asked her, "Do you think the charges are false?" "Certainly I believe they are false—absolutely," she said.[3]

Clinton elaborated further in an interview with Matt Lauer on NBC's *Today* show on January 27. She once again proclaimed her belief in her husband's innocence but also went a step further, blaming outside forces for what was happening. "This is—the great story here for anybody willing to find it and write about it and explain it is this vast right-wing conspiracy that has been conspiring against my husband since the day he announced for president."[4]

Vast right-wing conspiracy? There is a great deal of truth to that statement: For years, a number of her husband's conservative political enemies—politicians, lawyers, and publishers among others—had worked together to assist the Starr investigation. It is also true, however, that while these forces were trying to destroy the Clinton presidency, it was Bill Clinton himself who had had the inappropriate sexual relationship with Monica Lewinsky, giving his enemies the weapon they needed to bring him down.

The American public, while appalled by the president's private behavior, still supported him. Within a week of his wife's appearance on the *Today* show, polls showed that 59 percent of Americans believed that "Clinton's political enemies are conspiring to bring down his presidency."[5] For the time being at least, voters were standing behind their president.

Despite public support, the possibility grew that the president would be impeached. Starr told representatives of the House Judiciary Committee that evidence of obstruction of justice and perjury against the president was growing. He also felt that the president's actions were so demeaning to the office of the president that neither Congress nor the American people would want him to remain in office. Many Republicans, eager to take their political battles with the president to a new level, were itching to begin impeachment proceedings.

THE TRUTH COMES OUT

On August 6, Lewinsky told the grand jury her story of what happened between her and the president. Starr then issued a subpoena compelling the president to testify on August 17. The president was cornered. If he pleaded the Fifth Amendment before the grand jury, it would be political suicide. If he continued to deny the truth, voters would turn against him. If he acknowledged the truth, it would mean admitting to his wife that he had lied to her. There was only one option.

Once again, Hillary Clinton awoke to her husband telling her there was something he had to say. This time he told her the truth, saying that there had been an "inappropriate intimacy"[6] between him and Lewinsky. He said he could not tell her before because he was too ashamed and he knew how angry and hurt she would be. Hillary Clinton's reaction, as she remembered it in her autobiography, was not unexpected:

> I could hardly breathe. Gulping for air, I started crying and yelling at him, "What do you mean? What

are you saying? Why did you lie to me? I was furious and getting more so by the second. He just stood there saying over and over again, "I'm sorry. I'm so sorry. I was trying to protect you and Chelsea." I couldn't believe what I was hearing. Up until now I only thought that he'd been foolish for paying attention to the young woman and was convinced that he was being railroaded. I couldn't believe he would do anything to endanger our marriage and our family. I was dumbfounded, heartbroken, and outraged that I'd believed him at all.[7]

Two days later, President Bill Clinton gave four hours of testimony to the grand jury. He then prepared a speech to the country, apologizing for lying and misleading his family, friends, and the nation. Under normal circumstances, Hillary Clinton would have been his top adviser on such an important speech, but not that night. As she said in her autobiography, all she had to say to him was: "Well, Bill, this is your speech. You're the one who got yourself into this mess, and only you can decide what to say about it."[8]

The next morning, the Clintons, along with Chelsea, left Washington for their previously scheduled summer vacation on Martha's Vineyard. In news photos taken of their departure, Hillary Clinton is wearing dark glasses, her face unreadable, as Chelsea walked between her parents, holding hands with both. It was clearly a picture of a family in crisis.

Their vacation was a miserable time for everyone. The president slept downstairs in their borrowed house. Hillary Clinton slept upstairs. She could barely speak to her husband except to yell at him. He kept trying to explain and apologize, but she was not ready to be in the same room with him, much less forgive him. During the day, the president either played with his dog or met with advisers. The first lady spent time alone or talking with friends,

The Clintons, along with their dog, Buddy, walked from the White House toward a helicopter on August 18, 1998, as they left for a vacation in Martha's Vineyard, Massachusetts. The day before, President Clinton had testified to a grand jury about his relationship with former White House intern Monica Lewinsky.

trying to figure out what to do next. Her feelings of pain and of betrayal by her husband, the man she had loved for 27 years, were nearly unbearable.

As Clinton said in her autobiography, she would have to "go deep inside myself and my faith to discover any remaining belief in our marriage, to find some path to understanding."[9] By the end of August, after spending time alone as well as consulting with friends like her youth minister Don Jones, she decided that, despite her feelings of sadness and disappointment, she still loved her husband. While she wasn't sure if she was ready to fight for her husband and her marriage, she was determined to fight for her president. As she said in *Living History*:

> My personal feelings and political beliefs were on a collision course. As his wife, I wanted to wring Bill's neck. But he was not only my husband, he was also my president, and I thought that, in spite of everything, Bill led America and the world in a way that I continued to support. . . . I believe what my husband did was morally wrong. So was lying to me and misleading the American people about it. I also knew his failing was not a betrayal of his country.[10]

After returning from vacation, the Clintons began to slowly work through their problems. They attended marriage counseling, conferred with religious leaders, and spent time together talking, as Hillary Clinton worked through what had happened and decided whether to stay in the marriage. Gradually, she came to forgive her husband and decided that, because she still loved him, the marriage was worth saving. She said in her autobiography, "No one understands me better, and no one can make me laugh the way Bill does. Even after all these years, he is still the most interesting, energizing, and fully alive person I have ever met."[11]

Ironically, just seven years after she was criticized for her statements about Tammy Wynette and "Stand by Your Man," she was now living the song's lyrics:

> But if you love him, you'll forgive him
> Even though he's hard to understand
> And if you love him
> Oh be proud of him
> 'Cause after all he's just a man[12]

IMPEACHMENT AND POPULARITY

Hillary Clinton was not the only person in the United States standing behind Bill Clinton. Even after admitting his relationship with Lewinsky, President Clinton's approval ratings remained high. Apparently Starr was wrong: The American people had decided that the Lewinsky scandal, while wrong, was not enough to drive Bill Clinton from the White House. The economy was booming, the popularity of Newt Gingrich and the Republican Congress was dropping, and to the majority of Americans the sins of the president were a private matter between him and his wife. Of course, without his wife's support, it seems unlikely that his popularity would have stayed high. If she had walked out on him, so too would have the American people.

Interestingly, the only person more popular than the president was the first lady. By the end of 1998, her approval ratings had reached nearly 70 percent. These results must have seemed odd to her: After years of trying and failing to win the American people's respect and admiration by working hard, by attempting to bring health care to all, and by being a voice on human rights and her husband's most trusted adviser, it was only now after her husband had betrayed her and she had decided to stay with him that she had earned the public's respect.

Of course, not everybody agreed with that decision. Some people could not and would not accept the fact that she had stayed with her husband out of love—they felt that her decision to stay was driven by her own political ambitions. But, as Jeff Gerth and Don Van Natta Jr. point out in their book *Her Way*, "For the Americans who had disliked the first lady, some seemed to accept and even embrace Hillary the victim, finding that role far more appealing than Hillary the lawyer or Hillary the strategist or Hillary the feminist or Hillary the health-care savior."[13]

Ignoring the polls, the Republican-dominated House of Representatives decided to go ahead with impeachment proceedings against the president. Even after the mid-term

IMPEACHMENT IN THE UNITED STATES

Impeachment can be defined as a formal accusation issued by a legislature against a public official charged with a crime or other serious misconduct. In the United States, the right to impeach public officials is found in the Constitution in Article I, Sections 2 and 3, which discuss the procedure, and in Article II, Section 4, which states the grounds for impeachment: "The President, Vice President, and all civil officers of the United States shall be removed from office on impeachment for, and conviction of, treason, bribery, or other high crimes and misdemeanors."

Actually removing an official from office is a two-step process: (1) a formal accusation, or impeachment, from the House of Representatives, and (2) a trial and conviction by the Senate. Although impeachment requires only a simple majority vote by the House, conviction is much more difficult, requiring a two-thirds vote by the Senate.

The U.S Constitution was ratified in 1789, and the first impeachment, of Senator William Blount, occurred just 10 years later, in 1799. (Those charges were later dismissed.) The House has initiated impeachment proceedings only 62 times since 1789, with just 17 of those leading to actual impeachment. The ranks of those impeached include two presidents (Andrew Johnson and William Jefferson Clinton), a cabinet member (Secretary of War William W. Belknap in 1876), a senator (the aforementioned William Blount), a justice of the Supreme Court (Samuel Chase in 1805), and 11 federal judges. Of those, the Senate has convicted and removed only seven, all of them judges.

elections resulted in unexpected Democratic gains as voters made clear their displeasure with the intentions of the Republican Congress, the impeachment process began in earnest.

Most constitutional scholars agreed that the president's actions did not reach the standards of "treason, bribery, or other high crimes and misdemeanors" as laid out in the Constitution. Hillary Clinton, a veteran of the Nixon impeachment proceedings, also felt strongly that her husband's private behavior and effort to conceal it did not constitute a legal or historical basis for impeachment under the Constitution. The Republicans went ahead anyway. Carl Bernstein explained that the Republicans felt that they had nothing to lose by voting for impeachment and that such an attempt would only pay off for them in increased donations from the Republican base, who still hated the Clintons.

Hillary Clinton went on the offense, speaking publicly and privately to Democratic members of Congress, urging them to stand up and stay united behind their president. They did. On December 19, 1998, voting nearly on party lines, Clinton was impeached by the House of Representatives on grounds of perjury to a grand jury and obstruction of justice. Two months later, after a five-week Senate trial, Clinton was acquitted on both charges, with no Democrat voting to convict. After more than a year of headlines, the Monica Lewinsky scandal was over.

Bill Clinton's presidency had survived, and so had his marriage. The dynamics of the marriage, though, had changed: For more than 20 years, Hillary Rodham Clinton had been a faithful political spouse, supporting her husband's career at the expense of her own. Now, with Clinton's presidency in its last year, it was time for her to start planning her *own* career, independent of her husband's. It was time for her to restart the career she had put on hold 25 years earlier when she made the decision to follow her heart to Arkansas.

The New Senator
from New York

By the beginning of 1999, at the same time that her husband was on trial in the U.S. Senate, Hillary Clinton was already considering her political future. Senator Daniel Patrick Moynihan of New York had announced that he would not be seeking re-election. Many leading Democrats urged her to run for his seat. But Clinton was not sure what she wanted to do after she left the White House.

According to Carl Bernstein, running for public office on her own had never been part of Clinton's plan. Indeed, until she had gone out campaigning for Democrats in the 1998 mid-term elections, she had never truly felt comfortable on the stump. It was then, for the first time, that she felt herself truly connecting with her audiences as her own person, not just as the political wife of Bill Clinton.

On February 12, 1999, the very day that the Senate was voting "not guilty" on both articles of impeachment against her husband, Hillary Clinton sat down with adviser Harold Ickes, an expert on New York politics, to discuss the realities of running for the U.S. Senate. He began by pointing out that New York was a state with more than 19 million citizens, covering 54,000 square miles (140,000 square kilometers). To have any chance of winning, Clinton would have to learn the ins and outs of local politics, the cultures and economics of upstate New York, the suburbs, and New York City itself. For a political amateur, that alone would be a daunting challenge.

There was more. Clinton was not even a native New Yorker, had never lived in the state, had never run for office, and would in all likelihood face a tough Republican opponent in New York City Mayor Rudolph Giuliani. No woman had ever won statewide office in New York. The campaign would be brutal and nasty, with the national Republican Party doing all it could to defeat her politically once and for all. Was it worth going through all that?

Clinton did have other options. Friends argued that she would be more effective working in the international arena than as a member of the U.S. Senate. She had been approached about running foundations, becoming a college president or a corporate CEO—even hosting a television show! But the idea of running for office on her own was growing more and more attractive.

What persuaded her to run? Her husband's encouragement certainly played a part. He offered his full support, promising to help in any way he could. If she ran, their roles would now be reversed: Bill Clinton would be the supportive spouse. Hillary Clinton's desire to redeem her own legacy, to make up for the mistakes of her husband's administration, and to undo her own personal humiliation certainly all played a role in her decision as well.

In her autobiography, Clinton paints a picture of herself as undecided about running until she was at an event promoting an HBO special about women in sports entitled "Dare to Compete." She wrote:

> Sofia Totti, the captain of the girls' basketball team, introduced me. As I went to shake her hand, she leaned toward me and whispered in my ear.
>
> "Dare to compete, Mrs. Clinton," she said. "Dare to compete."[1]

That was all the encouragement she needed. Hillary Clinton soon announced her decision to run for the U.S. Senate, and she and her husband purchased a house in Chappaqua, New York. It was a unique situation: The first lady of the United States was also a candidate for public office.

Clinton immediately set out on what she labeled a "listening tour" of New York, traveling in a Ford conversion van, getting to know the state and its people. While she started out slowly, she gradually discovered herself as a candidate. Getting the Democratic nomination turned out to be simple: Every other major contender dropped out of the race as soon as Clinton announced. In mid-May, Hillary Clinton was formally nominated as the U.S. Senate candidate from New York. Her campaign had an additional lucky break early on when Rudolph Giuliani announced that he was withdrawing from the race due to health issues and news reports about his own extramarital affair. In his place, the Republicans nominated Rick Lazio, a little known congressman.

Lazio, with strong financial backing from the national Republican Party, attacked Clinton politically and personally, but with little success. On one occasion, during a televised debate, Lazio moved from behind his podium and walked over to hers, waving a piece of paper in his hand, demanding that she sign what he called the "New York Freedom from Soft Money Pact." While Lazio thought that it made him look strong and decisive, polls showed that voters, especially women, were offended by his bullying tactics.

He continued his negative campaigning, saying in a fundraising letter that his message could be summed up in six words: "I'm running against Hillary Rodham Clinton."[2] In other words, he wasn't running on what he wanted to do for New York; he was running solely on the fact that he was *not* Hillary Clinton.

The attacks did not work. On November 7, 2000, Hillary Clinton was elected to the U.S. Senate by a margin of 55 percent to 43 percent. It was the first time a first lady had ever been elected to public office. One month later, it was announced that she had signed an $8 million contract with Simon and Schuster to write a memoir of her years as first lady—the second-highest nonfiction book advance payment in history.

SENATOR HILLARY CLINTON

When Hillary Clinton entered the U.S. Senate, she was undoubtedly the best-known person there. It was expected that she would use her fame and media "star power" to gain immediate influence. Instead, she accepted her role as a freshman senator with unexpected grace and modesty.

The Senate is a club of just 100 people, each jealous of others' status and power. Learning from the mistakes she had made in the White House, Clinton played to them—never throwing her weight around, never being more than just another freshman senator. She made alliances with important senators on both sides of the aisle, even working with those who had voted to convict her husband in the impeachment trial. She became a regular member of the Senate Prayer Breakfast. She got coffee for her male colleagues. Other senators, even those who had been her sworn political enemies, began to have a new-found respect for her, referring to her as a workhorse, not a show horse.

In the aftermath of the September 11, 2001, terrorist attacks on New York City's World Trade Center, Clinton was at the forefront in seeking to obtain funding for the state's recovery efforts and security improvements. Indeed, for the most part, her efforts during her first term in office were targeted toward her state, as she sought to avoid controversy and keep a generally low profile. There was one vote, however, that has caused her political problems nearly from the outset: Her vote on the October 2002 Iraq War Resolution.

THE IRAQ WAR

On October 10, 2002, Senator Clinton, along with 28 other Democratic senators, voted to authorize President George W. Bush to use force against Iraq and Saddam Hussein. (21 other Democratic senators were opposed.) On that day, Clinton delivered a speech on the floor of the Senate explaining her vote. She said:

> This is a very difficult vote. This is probably the hardest decision I have ever had to make—any vote that may lead to war should be hard—but I cast it with conviction. . . . Perhaps my decision is influenced by my eight years of experience on the other end of Pennsylvania Avenue in the White House, watching my husband deal with serious challenges to our nation.[3]

Senator Clinton was one of the most ardent supporters of the war, at least at the outset. And while her reasons for supporting the war were many, one reason in particular stands out. It was obvious to most observers that at some point Hillary Clinton would be running for the presidency. For her to have any chance of success, she would have to prove that she was tough enough to be commander in chief, to be as tough if not tougher than any of her male counterparts.

If the war had gone as quickly and as easily as the Bush administration had promised, her vote would not have presented her with any political difficulties. But as the war continued and opposition to it grew, especially among fellow Democrats, she began to slowly back away from her initial support of the war. "I'm not going to believe this president again," she said on NBC's *Today* show on December 19, 2006. "Obviously, if we knew then what we know now, there wouldn't have been a vote, and I certainly wouldn't have voted that way."[4]

But in 2003, her vote, along with her successful campaign to ingratiate herself with her fellow senators, had paid off: She was appointed to a seat on the Armed Services Committee, a highly unusual honor for a first-term senator. Hillary Clinton, though, was obviously not a typical first-term senator. Her profile and stature was growing both within the Senate and nationwide. As an added bonus, her seat on the Armed Services Committee allowed her to gain military credentials that would be vital should she decide to run for the presidency.

She became a behind-the-scenes power within the Senate, helping to coordinate policy and to compete successfully with the Republicans in getting the Democrats' message out to the public. She also reached out to religious groups that had become the Republican Party's most reliable bloc of voters. Some in the Senate began to grumble that Clinton was amassing too much power, but her efforts did prove effective: In 2006, the percentage of the

Senator Hillary Clinton listened to testimony in August 2006 during a hearing before the Senate Armed Services Committee. Gaining a seat on the committee was rare for a first-term senator. Her national profile and stature were growing.

religious vote going to Republicans dropped significantly from the previous election. Within just her first term of office, Clinton had become one of the most effective and influential Democratic senators.

RE-ELECTION

To no one's surprise, in November 2004, Clinton announced that she would seek a second term in the United States Senate. But as 2005 turned into 2006, it became apparent that the Iraq War was going to be *the* issue for Democrats running for office. Clinton now found herself in the position of supporting an unpopular war. She had even been booed at a conference of liberal activists in June 2006, when she said that she did not think it was a smart strategy to set a deadline for withdrawal of U.S. troops from Iraq.

Just two weeks later, however, she took to the floor of the U.S. Senate, voicing her support for a bill that urged the administration to begin a phased deployment of U.S. troops from Iraq by the end of 2006. Although the bill failed to pass, Clinton gained credit for shifting her views on the war. She further bolstered her position with her tough questioning of Defense Secretary Donald Rumsfeld when he appeared before the Senate Armed Services Committee.

With her prior support for the war largely neutralized as an election issue, Clinton easily won the Democratic nomination for the Senate in New York, beating anti-war candidate Jonathan Tasini with 83 percent of the vote. She then went on to beat her Republican rival, former Yonkers Mayor John Spencer, with 67 percent of the vote, carrying all but four of New York's 62 counties.

Hillary Clinton, the junior senator from New York, was now one of the most widely known and admired of all Democratic politicians. Since 2002, she had been discussed as a possible presidential candidate. With the 2008 elections coming up, the time would soon come for her to announce her intentions.

The Run for the White House

Hillary Clinton was ranked No. 18 on *Forbes* magazine's list of the world's most powerful women in 2006, second only to Secretary of State Condoleezza Rice among U.S. government figures. She had become one of the Senate's most powerful and influential figures, rated by one Senate aide as "first among equals." It had long been assumed that at one point, sooner rather than later, she would make a run for president, thereby returning the Clintons to the White House and establishing herself as the primary partner in the couple's marriage. In addition, she would finally be living up to the expectations of many who had known her at Wellesley and had predicted that she would be the first woman president, years before she had put her own ambitions aside to help her husband achieve his.

On January 20, 2007, Hillary Clinton announced on her Web site the formation of a presidential exploratory committee (the usual first step in a candidacy), with the intention of becoming a candidate in 2008 for the office of president. In her announcement, she promised to bring "the right end" to the war in Iraq, reduce the deficit (which had grown again during the presidency of George W. Bush), make the country energy-independent, and provide affordable health care to all Americans. She said:

> After six years of George Bush, it is time to renew the promise of America. I grew up in a middle-class family in the middle of America, and we believed in that promise. I still do. I've spent my entire life trying to make good on it, whether it was fighting for women's basic rights or children's basic health care, protecting our Social Security or protecting our soldiers. . . . I'm in. And I'm in to win.[1]

She was entering a crowded field of Democratic contenders. By the time the list was complete, Clinton found herself facing eight other contenders; two of whom, Illinois Senator Barack Obama and former North Carolina Senator and 2004 vice presidential candidate John Edwards, were considered her strongest opponents.

Throughout most of 2007, Clinton led the field of candidates in opinion polls. She set leads in fundraising, and, backed up by the Clinton name and political machine as well as her experience and strong political record, many observers felt that she was a sure thing to become the first woman ever to be nominated by a major party for the office of president of the United States.

By September 2007, opinion polling in the first six states holding Democratic primaries or caucuses showed that Clinton was ahead in all of them. That same month, Clinton unveiled her American Choices Plan, an "individual mandate" universal health-care plan that would require health-care coverage for all individuals. Claiming that she had learned from her previous mistakes, Clinton emphasized that the plan involved no new government bureaucracy, but Republican opponents disagreed, immediately dubbing it "Hillary care 2.0" Regardless, an October poll taken by CNN showed Clinton with a lead of 51 percent to 21 percent over Obama, her closest rival. Leading in the polls, leading in fundraising, and with an earned reputation as a very solid debater who never made mistakes, it seemed to many that the Democratic presidential nomination was within her grasp. The problem, though, is that when you are leading the pack, you become the focus of all of your opponents.

In a Democratic debate held on October 30, 2007, in Philadelphia, Pennsylvania, Clinton was the subject of two hours of nearly continuous attacks from her Democratic rivals. And, unfortunately for Clinton, it was also the night when she made what was for her a rare series of mistakes— Roger Simon of *Politico* called it "the worst performance of her entire campaign."[2]

In the weeks following the debate, Clinton's poll numbers began to weaken, and by December 2007 the race between her and Obama had tightened, especially in the early caucus and primary states of Iowa, New Hampshire, and South Carolina. The Clinton camp, which had tried to create an image of her as the establishment candidate who was certain to win, grew concerned. Their problem was this: If you have been trying to convince voters that your candidate is unbeatable, and she is then beaten . . . what can you say after that?

THE FIRST VOTES

In the Iowa Democratic caucuses on January 3, 2008, Clinton was shocked to come in third place behind Obama and Edwards. Although the actual number of delegates was small, the loss was a major blow to Clinton's campaign in terms of damaging her image as the "inevitable" leader in the race and giving the Obama campaign considerable momentum.

The next primary stop was in New Hampshire, where according to most polls, Obama was pulling into the lead. Some political analysts were already predicting that, if Clinton lost in New Hampshire, her presidential hopes were over. Clinton fought back, attacking Obama and his promise to bring about "change," saying in the New Hampshire debate that "making change is not about what you believe; it's not about a speech you make. It's about working hard. . . . I'm not just running on a promise for change. I'm running on 35 years of change."[3]

But what may have had the most powerful impact on New Hampshire voters was a televised exchange between Clinton and a voter from Portsmouth, New Hampshire, who asked her, "How did you get out of the door every day? I mean, as a woman, I know how hard it is to get out of the house and get ready? Who does your hair?"[4] The question seemed to focus on the more mundane aspects of Clinton's day, but she chose to answer the question differently. Clinton had been on the defensive politically for weeks, facing attacks from all sides, and she answered the question as if it meant "How do you find the courage to keep doing what you're doing?" Clinton replied:

> I just don't want to see us fall backward as a nation. I mean, this is very personal for me. Not just political. I see what's happening. We have to reverse it. Some people think elections are a game: who's up or who's down. It's about our country. It's about our kids' future. It's about all of us together. Some of us put ourselves out there and do this against some difficult odds. . . . This is one of the most important

elections we'll ever face. So as tired as I am and as difficult as it is to keep up what I try to do on the road . . . I just believe . . . so strongly in who we are as a nation. I'm going to do everything I can to make my case, and then the voters get to decide.[5]

With this answer, her voice cracking and with tears in her eyes, Clinton let down the veil of privacy and strength she had always hidden behind. As a female candidate for president, she had felt the need to always project an image of strength and decisiveness. Now, for perhaps the first time as a candidate for president, she revealed part of who she really was, showing her long-held belief in herself as someone who could and would bring about positive change in people's lives.

It made a difference. Although seven polls had predicted a win for Obama in New Hampshire, Clinton won the primary with 39 percent of the vote compared with Obama's 36 percent. That night, Clinton spoke to her supporters, saying "I come tonight with a full heart. Over the last week, I listened to you, and in the process I found my own voice."[6] Many political pundits agreed that the reason for Clinton's surprising "comeback" was that her widely reported tearful response had "humanized" her and made her suddenly more likable.

Despite Clinton's New Hampshire victory, her road to the Democratic nomination was no longer a sure thing. Obama proved to be a much stronger candidate than anyone had anticipated, and the two battled it out across a nationwide system of primaries and caucuses.

Obama won the South Carolina primary on January 26. Clinton won nine out of the twenty-four states that held primaries or caucuses on February 5—Super Tuesday— including the delegate-rich prizes of California, New York, New Jersey, and Massachusetts. Obama won in

Hillary Clinton spoke with Laura Styles of Exeter, New Hampshire, in January 2008 during a campaign stop at a café in Portsmouth, New Hampshire. Earlier, Clinton had become emotional while answering a question from an undecided voter. Clinton won the New Hampshire primary, a victory she needed after a third-place finish in the Iowa caucuses.

the remaining 15 states that voted that day, as well as in Louisiana, Nebraska, and Washington four days later. Obama swept to several more victories in February, including in Virginia, Maryland, the District of Columbia, and Wisconsin. In early March, Clinton bounced back with victories in Ohio, Texas, and Rhode Island. It was a fierce political battle between two generations and between two voting blocs. Clinton's support largely came from older Americans, the working class, and from women, eager to see one of their own as president of the United States for the first time in history. Obama's support came from younger voters, more educated voters, and from African Americans, also eager to see one of *their* own become president of the United States for the first time in history. Indeed, it would be a historic outcome—a female nominee or an African-American nominee—no matter who ultimately won.

THE PRESIDENTIAL NOMINATING PROCESS

The series of presidential primary elections and caucuses is one of the first steps in the process of electing the president of the United States. The primary elections are run by state and local governments. Caucuses are private events run by the two main political parties—the Democrats and the Republicans. A state primary election or caucus usually determines how many delegates to each party's national convention each candidate will receive from that state. Then, at the national convention, the candidate who receives the majority of votes from the delegates becomes his or her party's nominee for president.

It is interesting that there is no provision for the role of political parties in the U.S. Constitution. Historically, presidential nominees had been selected by delegates chosen at district conventions, usually by party bosses—voters had little or no say in the process. In 1910, Oregon became the first state to establish a presidential preference primary. By 1912, 12 states either selected delegates in primaries, used a preferential primary, or both. By 1920, the number of states with primaries had risen to 20.

By the middle of March 2008, Clinton, for the first time in her own political career, found herself facing defeat. She was behind Obama in delegates to the Democratic convention, as well as in the popular vote. Mathematically at least, with just 10 states left to vote, it seemed virtually impossible for Clinton to surpass or even catch up with Obama and obtain the 2,024 delegates necessary to win

But it was the chaotic 1968 Democratic National Convention that was the impetus for national adoption of the binding primary election. There, Vice President Hubert Humphrey won the nomination despite a series of primary victories by Senator Eugene McCarthy, an anti-Vietnam War candidate. After this, a panel led by Senator George McGovern recommended that states adopt new rules to assure wider participation by voters. A large number of states chose the presidential primary as the best way to observe the new Democratic Party rules. The result was that many more delegates would be selected by state presidential primaries. The Republicans soon followed suit, adopting many more state presidential primaries of their own.

With more and more states having presidential primaries, states began to try to increase their influence by moving their primaries earlier and earlier on the calendar. One result of this was February 5, 2008, when 24 states and American Samoa held primaries or caucuses for one or both parties. Attempts have been made to reform the primary process, to make it more fair and representative, but to date, getting the states to agree has been an impossible task.

the nomination. A growing number of leading Democrats urged her to withdraw from the race, saying that it was necessary for the party to unite behind Obama. She refused to surrender.

If there's anything that is certain about Hillary Clinton, it's that she is not a quitter. She refused to give up after her husband had been defeated for re-election as governor, she refused to give up when the Gennifer Flowers scandal threatened to derail his 1992 presidential campaign, and she refused to give up when her husband's presidency was threatened by the Monica Lewinsky affair. She was not about to surrender her own political aspirations before every vote had been cast, before every possible path to victory was tried.

Clinton still had two hopes remaining. If she could win the remaining primaries convincingly, she might be able to persuade more so-called superdelegates—delegates not bound by the results of any primary or caucus—to give their support to her, winning her the nomination. Also still to be resolved were the results of the Michigan and Florida primaries. Clinton had won both states by convincing margins, but because they had rescheduled their primaries for dates earlier in the year in defiance of Democratic Party rules, the results of those primaries were not being counted. If those delegations could be seated, or if it were possible for new primaries to be held, it was still possible for Clinton to catch Obama and get the nomination. The next few months would be decisive.

FIGHTING TILL THE END

Indeed, it was in the last months of the Democratic primary battle that Clinton found her voice. She began to reach out to white working-class voters, presenting herself as their ally, as someone who understood their problems; and they responded in droves. Clinton won nine of the last fourteen primaries, including the important battleground states of Pennsylvania and Ohio. But it was too late.

The lead that Obama had run up early in the race was insurmountable. By the beginning of May, it became apparent to nearly all observers that it was virtually impossible for Clinton to wrestle the nomination away from Obama. Pressure mounted for Clinton to withdraw from the race, but as she had shown throughout her life, she was most tenacious in battle when her back was against a wall. Clinton held on through the last Democratic primary of the season, fighting for every vote and hoping that the superdelegates, impressed by her demonstrated strength among white working-class voters, would throw their support to her. But it was not to be. Since Obama had won the most delegates in the primaries and caucuses, the superdelegates endorsed Obama as well.

On June 7, Hillary Rodham Clinton conceded to Barack Obama in a speech at the National Building Museum in Washington, D.C. After endorsing her rival for the Democratic nomination, she reflected on the historic nature of her campaign: No female candidate had ever received as many votes, more than 18 million in total, or had won as many primaries. Once again, she had blazed a trail for women throughout the country. She said:

> From now on it will be . . . unremarkable to think a woman could be president of the United States. And that is truly remarkable. . . . Although we weren't able to shatter that highest, hardest glass ceiling this time, thanks to you, it's got about 18 million cracks in it.[7]

Her millions of supporters held out hope that Obama would choose her to run with him as vice president, but the long primary season had done its damage. In the end,

Speaking at the Democratic National Convention on August 26, 2008, Hillary Clinton urged the crowd to give its support to the Democratic ticket. After a lengthy primary season, Clinton had lost the Democratic nomination for president to Barack Obama.

Obama chose Senator Joseph Biden of Delaware to be his running mate. In a stirring speech at the 2008 Democratic National Convention in Denver, Colorado, Clinton gave her unqualified endorsement and support to the Democratic ticket and went on to speak words that were both universal and yet deeply personal:

> My mother was born before women could vote. My daughter got to vote for her mother for president. This is the story of women and men who defy the odds and never give up. How do we give this country back to them? By following the example of a brave New Yorker, a woman who risked her life to bring slaves along the Underground Railroad. On that path to freedom, Harriet Tubman had one piece of advice. If you hear the dogs, keep going. If you see the torches in the woods, keep going. If they're shouting after you, keep going. Don't ever stop. Keep going. If you want a taste of freedom, keep going. And even in the darkest of moments, that is what Americans have done. We have found the faith to keep going.[8]

And that, of course, is exactly what Hillary Rodham Clinton has always done. She has kept going. She has persevered. That determination will serve Clinton well as she takes on her next challenge. After his victory in November, President-elect Obama named Clinton to be his secretary of state—the chief diplomat for the administration. Her renown and her credibility are considered assets as Obama seeks to repair relations with U.S. allies and negotiate with the country's foes. So, despite her loss in the presidential race, this remarkable woman—a longtime champion of the rights of women and children—will not be leaving the international stage anytime soon.

1947   Born on October 26 in Chicago, Illinois, to Hugh Rodham, the owner of a textile business, and Dorothy Rodham, a homemaker.

1950   Moves to Park Ridge, Illinois.

1964   Becomes a "Goldwater Girl," volunteering for the presidential campaign of Republican Barry Goldwater.

1965   Enters Wellesley College, graduating in 1969 with a degree in political science; here, her political beliefs evolve from conservative to liberal.

1969   Attends Yale Law School, where she meets Bill Clinton, graduating in 1973.

1974   After her work for the U.S. House of Representatives impeachment inquiry ends, Hillary Rodham moves to Arkansas, where Bill Clinton's political career is just beginning.

1975   Hillary Rodham marries Bill Clinton on October 11, keeping her last name.

1977   Becomes an associate at Rose Law Firm.

1979   Bill Clinton begins his first term as governor; Hillary Rodham is named a partner at Rose Law Firm; she would twice be named as one of the 100 most influential lawyers in the United States by the *National Law Journal*.

1982   Bill Clinton wins back the governorship he lost in 1980; Hillary Rodham adds her husband's last name, becoming Hillary Rodham Clinton.

1992   Bill Clinton wins the presidency.

1993–1994   Hillary Clinton heads the President's Task Force on National Health Care Reform; facing certain political defeat, the bill is never introduced to the full Senate.

1994   Kenneth Starr is appointed in August as special counsel to investigate the Clintons' dealings with Whitewater.

1995   Hillary Clinton makes a major speech on women's rights at the United Nations' Fourth World Conference on Women in Beijing.

1996   Bill Clinton is re-elected president; Hillary Clinton publishes *It Takes a Village*.

1998–1999   Monica Lewinsky scandal: President Clinton is impeached by the U.S. House of Representatives but is acquitted by the Senate on February 12, 1999.

2000   Hillary Clinton is elected to the U.S. Senate from New York.

2002   Senator Clinton votes to authorize President George W. Bush to use force against Iraq.

2003   Publishes her autobiography, *Living History*.

2006   Re-elected to the U.S. Senate.

2007   **January 20** Announces her campaign to run for U.S. president.

2008   During the first half of the year, Hillary Clinton battles with Senator Barack Obama to win the Democratic presidential nomination.
June 7 Ultimately, Obama's early victories prove difficult to overcome, and Hillary Clinton concedes the nomination to him.
December 1 President-elect Obama nominates Hillary Clinton to be secretary of state.

NOTES

CHAPTER 1: FOLLOWING HER HEART

1. Hillary Rodham Clinton, *Living History*. New York: Simon and Schuster, 2003, p. 41.
2. Carl Bernstein, *A Woman in Charge: The Life of Hillary Rodham Clinton*. New York: Vintage Books, 2008, p. 61.
3. Clinton, *Living History*, p. 70.
4. "Hillary Clinton in Quotes." *Against Hillary Clinton* Web site. Available online at http://www.againsthillary.com/2007/07/19/hillary-clinton-in-quotes.
5. Elizabeth Kolbert, "The Lady Vanishes," *New Yorker*. June 11, 2007. Available online at http://www.newyorker.com/arts/critics/books/2007/06/11/070611crbo_books_kolbert?currentPage=2).
6. Clinton, *Living History*, p. 1.

CHAPTER 2: THE EARLY YEARS

1. Clinton, *Living History*, p. 2.
2. Bernstein, *A Woman in Charge*, p. 15.
3. Ibid., p. 13.
4. Clinton, *Living History*, p. 14.
5. Ibid., p. 12.
6. Ibid., p. 20.
7. Ibid., p. 13.
8. Bernstein, *A Woman in Charge*, p. 30.
9. Ibid, p. 30.
10. Clinton, *Living History*, p. 21.
11. Bernstein, *A Woman in Charge*, p. 34.
12. Clinton, *Living History*, p. 22.
13. Bernstein, *A Woman in Charge*, p. 34.

CHAPTER 3: CHANGING

1. Ibid., p. 41.
2. Clinton, *Living History*, p. 29.
3. Ibid., p. 27.
4. Bernstein, *A Woman in Charge*, p. 50.
5. Ibid., p. 50.
6. Ibid., p. 53.
7. Ibid., p. 54
8. Clinton, *Living History*, p. 36.
9. Ibid., p. 38.
10. Bernstein, *A Woman in Charge*, pp. 58–59.
11. Clinton, *Living History*, p. 41.
12. Bernstein, *A Woman in Charge*, p. 59.
13. Ibid., p. 59.
14. Clinton, *Living History*, p. 43.

CHAPTER 4: LAW AND BILL CLINTON AT YALE

1. Bernstein, *A Woman in Charge*, p. 63.
2. Clinton, *Living History*, p. 50.
3. Ibid., p. 52.
4. Bernstein, *A Woman in Charge*, p. 79.
5. Clinton, *Living History*, p. 52.
6. Ibid., p. 53.
7. Ibid., p. 53.
8. Bernstein, *A Woman in Charge*, pp. 81–82.
9. Ibid., p. 76.
10. Clinton, *Living History*, pp. 53–54.
11. Bernstein, *A Woman in Charge*, p. 82.
12. Clinton, *Living History*, p. 55.
13. Ibid., pp. 56–57.
14. Ibid., p. 57.
15. Bernstein, *A Woman in Charge*, p. 85.
16. Ibid., p. 86.
17 Ibid., pp. 85–86.
18. Ibid., p. 86.
19. Ibid., p. 87
20. Clinton, *Living History*, p. 61.
21. Ibid., p. 64
22. Bernstein, *A Woman in Charge*, pp. 93–94.
23. Ibid., p. 106.
24. Clinton, *Living History*, p. 69.
25. Ibid., p. 69.
26. Bernstein, *A Woman in Charge*, p. 107.

CHAPTER 5: LIFE IN ARKANSAS

1. Ibid., p. 109.
2. Clinton, *Living History*, p. 74.
3. Bernstein, *A Woman in Charge*, pp. 124–125.
4. Tamar Lewin, "Legal Scholars See Distortion in Attacks on Hillary Clinton," *New York Times*, August 24, 1992. Available online at http://query.nytimes.com/fullpage.html?res=9E0CEFD71E3EF937A1575BC0A964958260.
5. Garry Wills, "H.R. Clinton's Case," *New York Review of Books*, March 5, 1992.
6. Bernstein, *A Woman in Charge*, p. 141.
7. Clinton, *Living History*, pp. 83–84.
8. Ibid., p. 85.

CHAPTER 6: TWO FOR THE PRICE OF ONE

1. Ibid., p. 102.
2. Ibid., p. 105.
3. Bernstein, *A Woman in Charge*, p. 201.
4. Clinton, *Living History*, p. 107.
5. Ibid., p. 107.
6. Bernstein, *A Woman in Charge*, p. 202.
7. Clinton, *Living History*, p. 109.
8. Bernstein, *A Woman in Charge*, p. 207.
9. Ibid., p. 213.
10. Ibid., p. 284.

CHAPTER 7: HOPE AND DESPAIR

1. Bernstein, *A Woman in Charge*, pp. 254–255.
2. Clinton, *Living History*, p. 189.
3. Bernstein, *A Woman in Charge*, p. 396.
4. Clinton, *Living History*, p. 230.
5. Bernstein, *A Woman in Charge*, p. 401.
6. Ibid., p. 357.
7. Ibid., p. 409.
8. Joe Klein, "How Hillary Learned to Trust Herself," *Time*, January 9, 2008. Available online at http://www.time.com/time/politics/article/0,8599,1702043,00.html.
9. Clinton, *Living History*, p. 302.
10. Ibid., p. 305.
11. Ibid., p. 306.
12. Bernstein, *A Woman in Charge*, p. 438.
13. Ibid., p. 445.
14. Clinton, *Living History*, pp. 330–331.
15. Ibid., p. 375.
16. Ibid., p. 376.

CHAPTER 8: TESTED

1. Ibid., p. 341.
2. Jeff Gerth and Don Van Natta Jr., *Her Way: The Hopes and Ambitions of Hillary Rodham Clinton*. New York: Little Brown, 2007, p. 177.
3. Ibid., p. 178.
4. Bernstein, *A Woman in Charge*, p. 498.
5. Ibid., p. 503.
6. Clinton, *Living History*, p. 466.
7. Ibid., p. 466.
8. Ibid., p. 468.

9.   Ibid., p. 469.
10. Ibid., p. 471.
11. Ibid., p. 75.
12. Tammy Wynette, "Stand by Your Man."
13. Gerth and Van Natta, *Her Way*, p. 195.

CHAPTER 9: THE NEW SENATOR FROM NEW YORK

1.   Clinton, *Living History*, p. 501.
2.   Ibid., p. 521.
3.   Bernstein, *A Woman in Charge*, p. 549.
4.   Alex Koppelman and Jonathan Vanian, "What Hillary Clinton Should Have Known, *Salon*, February 26, 2007. Available online at http://www.salon.com/news/feature/2007/02/26/clinton_aumf.

CHAPTER 10: THE RUN FOR THE WHITE HOUSE

1.   "Hillary Clinton Launches White House Bid: 'I'm In,'" CNN.com, January 20, 2007. Available online at http://www.cnn.com/2007/POLITICS/01/20/clinton.announcement/index.html.
2.   Roger Simon, "Obama, Edwards Attack; Clinton Bombs Debate," *Politico*, October 31, 2007. Available online at http://www.politico.com/news/stories/1007/6634.html.
3.   Mark Mermott and Jill Lawrence, "Edwards: He and Obama Share a 'Conviction Alliance,'" *USA Today*, January 6, 2008. Available online at http://blogs.usatoday.com/onpolitics/2008/01/edwards-he-obam.html.
4.   Karen Breslau, "Hillary Tears Up," *Newsweek*, January 7, 2008. Available online at http://www.newsweek.com/id/85609/output/print.
5.   Ibid.
6.   Jennifer Parker, "Clinton Wins in N.H.: I 'Found My Voice,'" ABC News, January 9, 2008. Available online at http://abcnews.go.com/Politics/Vote2008/story?id=41033398page=1.
7.   "Hillary's Remarks in Washington, D.C.," June 7, 2008. Available online at http://www.hillaryclinton.com/news/speech/view/?id=7903.
8.   "Clinton: It Is Time to Take Back the Country We Love," CNN.com, August 26, 2008. Available online at http://www.cnn.com/2008/POLITICS/08/26/clinton.transcript/index.html.

BIBLIOGRAPHY

"A Short History of Impeachment," Infoplease. Available online at http://print.infoplease.com/spot/impeach.html.

"Barry Goldwater." Available online at http://www.spartacus.schoolnet.co.uk/USAgoldwater.htm.

Bernstein, Carl. *A Woman in Charge: The Life of Hillary Rodham Clinton*. New York: Vintage Books, 2008.

Breslau, Karen. "Hillary Tears Up." *Newsweek*, January 7, 2008. Available online at http://www.newsweek.com/id/85609/output/print.

Clinton, Hillary Rodham. *Living History*. New York: Simon and Schuster, 2003.

"Clinton: It Is Time to Take Back the Country We Love." CNN.com. August 26, 2008. Available online at http://www.cnn.com/2008/POLITICS/08/26/clinton.transcript/index.html.

"Eleanor Roosevelt Biography," Franklin D. Roosevelt Presidential Library and Museum. Available online at http://www.fdrlibrary.marist.edu/erbio.html.

Gerth, Jeff and Don Van Natta Jr. *Her Way: The Hopes and Ambitions of Hillary Rodham Clinton*. New York: Little Brown, 2007.

"Hillary Clinton in Quotes." *Against Hillary Clinton* Web site. Available online at http://www.againsthillary.com/2007/07/19/hillary-clinton-in-quotes.

"Hillary Clinton Launches White House Bid: 'I'm In.'" CNN.com. January 20, 2007. Available online at http://www.cnn.com/2007/POLITICS/01/20/clinton.announcement/index.html.

"Hillary Rodham Clinton Quotes." About.com. Available online at http://womenshistory.about.com/cs/quotes/a/qu_h_clinton.htm.

"Hillary's Remarks in Washington, D.C." June 7, 2008. Available online at http://www.hillaryclinton.com/news/speech/view/?id=7903.

Klein, Joe. "How Hillary Learned to Trust Herself." *Time*, January 9, 2008. Available online at http://www.time.com/time/politics/article/0,8599,1702043,00.html.

Kolbert, Elizabeth. "The Lady Vanishes." *New Yorker*, June 11, 2007. Available online at http://www.newyorker.com/arts/critics/books/2007/06/11/070611crbo_books_kolbert?currentPage=2)

Koppelman, Alex, and Jonathan Vanian. "What Hillary Should Have Known." *Salon*, February 26, 2007. Available online at http://www.salon.com/news/feature/2007/02/26/clinton_aumf/.

Lewin, Tamar. "Legal Scholars See Distortion in Attacks on Hillary Clinton." *New York Times*, August 24, 1992. Available online at

http://query.nytimes.com/fullpage.html?res=9E0CEFD71E3EF937A157
5BC0A964958260.

Mermott, Mark, and Jill Lawrence. "Edwards: He and Obama Share a 'Conviction Alliance.'" *USA Today*, January 6, 2008. Available online at http://blogs.usatoday.com/onpolitics/2008/01/edwards-he-obam.html.

Parker, Jennifer. "Clinton Wins in N.H.: I 'Found My Voice.'" ABC News, January 9, 2008. Available online at http://abcnews.go.com/Politics/Vote2008/story?id=41033398page=1.

Schneider, Bill. "Poll: As Thompson's Star Fades, Clinton's on the Rise." CNN.com, October 16, 2007. Available online at http://www.cnn.com/2007/POLITICS/10/16/schneider.poll/index.html.

Simon, Roger. "Obama, Edwards Attack; Clinton Bombs Debate." *Politico*, October 31, 2007. Available online at http://www.politico.com/news/stories/1007/6634.html.

Wills, Garry. "H.R. Clinton's Case." *New York Review of Books*, March 5, 1992.

Wynette, Tammy, "Stand by Your Man." Available online at www.lyricscafe.com/w/wynette_tammy/tammy04.html.

FURTHER RESOURCES

BOOKS

Bedell Smith, Sally. *For Love of Politics: Bill and Hillary Clinton: The White House Years*. New York: Random House, 2007.

Clinton, Bill. *My Life*. New York: Vintage Books, 2005.

Clinton, Hillary Rodham. *It Takes a Village, 10th Anniversary Edition*. New York: Simon and Schuster, 2006.

Clinton, Hillary Rodham. *An Invitation to the White House: At Home with History*. New York: Simon and Schuster, 2000.

Lash, Joseph. *Eleanor and Franklin: The Story of Their Relationship Based on Eleanor Roosevelt's Private Papers*. New York: W.W. Norton and Company, 1971.

WEB SITES

Hillary
   http://www.hillaryclinton.com

Hillary Clinton's Facebook page
   http://www.facebook.com/hillaryclinton

Hillary Clinton's MySpace page
   http://www.myspace.com/hillaryclinton

The U.S. Congress Votes Database: Hillary Clinton
   http://projects.washingtonpost.com/congress/members/c001041

INDEX

ABOUT THE AUTHOR

DENNIS ABRAMS is the author of several books for Chelsea House, including biographies of Barbara Park, Hamid Karzai, Albert Pujols, and Jay-Z. He attended Antioch College, where he majored in English and communications. A voracious reader since the age of three, Dennis lives in Houston, Texas, with his partner of 20 years, along with their two cats and their dog, Junie B.

PICTURE CREDITS

Page